"The authors have undertaken a Herculean task, documenting the history of the development of the environmental movement and its subsequent decline into a morass of government overkill. The Taking *is a "must" for anyone concerned with government intrusion into the private sector management of our natural resources. It is an invaluable guide to the history of the decline of private property rights in America."*

Mrs. Carol Hallett
Republican Minority Leader
of the California State Assembly

"I am deeply impressed with *The Taking* and its success in bringing a very important point of view to the American public."

Richard G. Lugar
United States Senator

The Taking

The Taking

Joseph Gughemetti

and

Eugene D. Wheeler

Hidden House Publications
Palo Alto, California

Acknowledgments

We acknowledge our gratitude to clients and professional colleagues with whom we shared experiences on a number of cases described in this book. We thank the many city, county, state, regional, and federal agency officials, including the staffs of the California Coastal Commission and the President's Council on Environmental Quality, who provided us with valuable information and data. We also want to express our appreciation to the numerous individuals and organizations for providing significant advice, including: Charles "Chuck" Cushman and the National Inholders Association; Gary Koeppel, former publisher of the Big Sur Gazette; Joe Owens of Congressman Lagomarsino's office; Westchester-Putnam Builders Institute; the National Association of Homebuilders; and especially the California Coastal Council, which led the fight against abuses of the California Coastal Commission. A special acknowledgment is given to Mr. Ric Davidge, the present chairman of the federal Land Policy group. He has for years been dedicated to achieving balanced federal land policies. More than any other person, Ric has been responsible for bringing the federal land issues to legislative consciousness and paving the way for a new and more equitable federal direction.

We owe special gratitude to our secretary, Lou Hartney, for her fine work, to Kathleen Wheeler for her editing, and to Eugenie Wheeler for her moral support.

Joseph Gughemetti and Eugene D. Wheeler

Copyright © Hidden House Publications, 1981.
All rights reserved.

ISBN: 0-8256-3861-5

Hidden House Publications
2698 Marine Way
Mountain View, California 94043

This book is dedicated to the victims of takings.

Contents

Preface

How does one challenge the environmental movement without being labeled an antienvironmentalist? How does one reveal a series of disturbing events that make one question fundamental precepts of a movement seemingly above criticism? It is difficult to envision an American who does not harbor a sincere concern for the protection of our natural resources and the quality of our environment. Yet it is just as difficult to envision an American who would not be disturbed by the events disclosed in this book.

Coauthors Joseph Gughemetti and Eugene Wheeler bring a particular expertise to this subject as, respectively, a land-use trial attorney and a land-use consultant, whose experiences with many of the victims led to their investigative analysis of the environmental movement.

The initial investigation around which this book was built centered in a series of local land-use abuses in California and expanded into a national analysis of a trend that alarmed the authors. This alarm was intensified by the apparent effects of excessive and unreasonable environmental regulations and their corresponding *hidden* costs upon consumers, taxpayers, and the housing market. Alarm was soon replaced by anger, as countless violations of civil and constitutional rights of American citizens by government bureaucracies were uncovered by the authors. Through their experiences, the authors gained a perspective and sense of the significance and impact of this trend.

The Taking was not written as an attack upon the legitimate goals of the environmental movement, goals that we all share. However, it *was* written to tell the story of the victims of the abuses of the movement and its legal processes and to tell the story of the terrifying precedential impact they have upon our future.

Chapter One

The Victims

When the rural American colonies declared their independence on July 4, 1776, they did so in affirmation of individual liberty, private property, and local government autonomy. The American Revolution that followed, often categorized as a movement for freedom of speech, religion, and local government, was also an assertion of private property rights. A decade after that revolution, those concepts were institutionalized by a constitutional guarantee that no citizen could "be deprived of life, liberty, or property without due process of law; nor shall private property be taken for public use without just compensation."

Over the next two centuries rural America was transformed into an industrial urban society of enormous material wealth. Yet the same society which created a standard of living without historic parallel also caused increasing deterioration of the air, water, and land resources of the American continent. The environmental degradation which could not be envisioned by rural colonial farmers became a natural aftermath to urban and industrial growth. The urban concentration of automobile and industrial emissions and sewage disposal caused major deterioration to air and water quality standards, and poorly conceived urban development increasingly usurped and wasted our most important natural resource: land.

The environmental movement emerged as a necessary reaction to excessive and poorly planned industrial and urban growth. The movement soon manifested itself in a series of government programs and regulations designed to enhance the quality of air and water, and preserve invaluable natural resources through public acquisition of private properties. It would be difficult to underestimate the contribution and value of the environmental movement to the quality of life in America. Yet just as the American industrial revolution experienced the victimization of the American Indian, the environmental movement has left a myriad of victims in its wake.

What began as a sincere and necessary concern for environmental standards became a billion dollar bureaucratic machine, often unrestrained, excessive, and unreasonable. The environmental issue was captured by bureaucracies and regulations with little concern for democratic procedures and often without a sense of reason, balance, or justice. This is the story of that effect, and of the "victims" of that movement: private enterprise, local government, and individuals. In "saving" the environment the movement challenged the very basis of our foundation and transformed a bold and decent goal into a gigantic bureaucratic excess.

The victims represent all sectors of American society, rich and poor alike, business, labor, industry, agriculture, and local government. For one moment in history they share a common injury, as victims of excessive federal and state regulations and unrestrained bureaucracies . . . and they come from every area of America.

The Indians of 1978

"We're the Indians of 1978," shouted Charles Cushman, head of the recently formed National Inholders Association, a group of landowners located within or adjoining the boundaries of federal parks throughout the United States. Cushman, a mountain man and former Yosemite Park resident, listed extensive examples of harassment of inholders throughout the country, including Grand Teton National Park, St. Croix, Cape Cod, Fire Island, Blue Ridge Parkway, and Yosemite. He spoke of the federal park directive to remove all private landowners from federal park areas and the radical implementation procedures of the federal authorities. He described the 76-year-old resident of Yosemite who was warned that his cabin and lifelong home would be taken by the federal government if he proceeded with attempts to add a bathroom; the miner in Death Valley who was threatened by federal park rangers with shotguns for mining on his own property; and the acquisition of entire towns, churches, homes, and schools by the federal authorities, which were then boarded up and left to deteriorate.

Big Sur, California

Victoria Consiglio, a 55-year-old housewife, had emigrated from Germany in pursuit of her father's advise that "the United States had the best constitution in the world." In 1976, Victoria and her husband invested their life savings in a two-acre residential lot along the majestic Big Sur coastline in California where they planned to build a one-bedroom retirement home. On October 22, 1979, after Victoria had obtained local building permit approvals, the California Coastal Commission (a state agency) refused to allow her to build, saying that the home would be visible to the public. In a ten-minute hearing, a $200,000 homesite had been reduced to a valueless preserve and a life savings destroyed. "I believe that what's happening to me now can't happen under this constitution. Nobody believes me when I tell them what's happened to me. . . . They say it can't happen. Well, it did."

Otter Cove (Carmel), California

A few miles north of Big Sur, near Carmel, California, the California Coastal Commission required a homeowner to camouflage his home from public view by covering the roof with 250 tons of earth and poison oak (to prevent trespassers). The commission felt that the motorists along the coast highway should not have their views cluttered with the sight of a home despite the existence of neighboring conventional homes in full view.

Blue Ridge Parkway, Virginia

In a resort community located near the Blue Ridge Parkway in Virginia, plans for a recreational resort community of 4,000 residential units, a golf course, and a ski slope remain only a faint memory. In 1973, the National Park Service contended that the sole access road to the community from the Blue Ridge Parkway was a traffic hazard and proceeded with highway alterations leading to an eventual denial of direct access. The court battles that ensued formed but a backdrop for the public outrage from the community of landowners. In effect, the government took property away from individuals by denying their access to it. At a public hearing before the National Park Service, a resident of the area compared the government's interference with another government, which had taken her parents' property:

It wasn't the Blue Ridge Parkway, and it wasn't a bureaucrat named * * * or a political appointee like * * *; their [her parents] property was in Warsaw, Poland, and it was a tyrant by the name of Joseph Stalin who took their property away. My father is dying a slow death to see that his daughter's property is being taken by his government.[1]

Alaska Wilderness

President Carter declared the Alaska Wilderness Bill to be one of the major environmental accomplishments of his administration. But for the residents of Alaska a different attitude prevails. The Alaskans had already experienced the disruptive efforts of "environmentalists" who blocked the Prudhoe Bay oil pipeline for ten years on the assumption that its existence would upset the caribou migrations. The caribou adjusted easily to the pipeline. The citizens of Alaska did not, however, adjust to federal control and environmental causes.

The Alaska Wilderness Bill set aside a wilderness preserve of over 105 million acres (one fourth of all federal land), an area approximately the same size as the state of California, banning or severely curtailing mineral exploration. This action created a wilderness area five times larger than all the combined wilderness areas in the continental United States, and permanently locked up sixteen–eighteen minerals considered vital to national security, including a substantial percentage of the total remaining coal, oil, and natural reserves of the country. A newspaper editorial described the administration's plan as one that was "drafted under the guise of preserving land for the public, but in fact makes land accessible only to an elite group of rich environmentalists who have the time, money, and stamina to facilitate excursions the average tourist cannot afford." Through this action, the State of Alaska, already 95 percent federally owned, was precluded from its own economic future, while the nation became more dependent upon foreign energy sources and the international abrasions of the Middle East.

Marina del Rey, California

In August 1979, the California Coastal Commission approved the permit applications of two proposed hotels in the exclusive luxury resort area of Marina del Rey in Los Angeles County. Although both hotels passed environmental considerations, the commission made its approval conditional upon social mandates. The first hotel was to reserve 45 of its 300 luxury rooms for occupancy by low and moderate income people on weekends at a cost of 50 percent of the published room rates. Construction of the second hotel was conditioned upon all of its 200 rooms being priced at rates linked to the published rates of a Motel 6 chain (low-priced units), the construction of a 50-bed hostel approved by the Youth Hostel Association of America, and the limitation of food prices to those of a Sambo's Restaurant (low priced). In the name of the environment, resort accommodations had been mandated for the poor.

Monterey, California

The Briggs trial created substantial controversy in the plush ocean community of Carmel, California. Three months of trial, twenty expert witnesses, and over $200,000 in court costs resulted in a verdict against the State of California. The trial judge signed fifty-five findings showing a conspiracy by state government officials of the Department of Parks and Recreation and California Coastal Commission to destroy the use of property belonging to a Mrs. Briggs. Evidence documented a subtle conspiracy by which the Briggs property had been denied all use and marketability pending formal condemnation by the State of California—a condemnation that did not thereafter occur.

The property was a high priority on the State of California's park acquisition list. The court reviewed the secret telegrams and nondisclosed communications between state officials, who in public opposed Briggs' modest three-home development attempts on the grounds of "environmental considerations," but in private orchestrated a ban on use of the property in order to freeze it for public acquisition.

The Fifth Amendment to the United States Constitution had been violated, for Briggs' property had been effectively taken *without* payment of just compensation. In October 1979, six years after the first government interference with the property, an appellate court reversed Briggs' $6.5 million judgment against the State of California and ruled as a matter of law that no action by the Department of Parks and Recreation could give rise to liability and damages; in effect, they ruled that *the constitution could be violated in the name of the environment.*

Goodyear Company

In the October 28, 1980 issue of the *Wall Street Journal,* an article on the decline of America's productivity growth delineated problems experienced by the Goodyear Tire and Rubber Company resulting from environmental regulations. In one week the company's computer center "cranked out 345,000 pages of jargon-filled paper weighing 3,200 pounds—all to meet one new regulation of the Occupational Safety and Health Administration."

The Goodyear Company calculated that "complying with regulations of six of the more demanding federal agencies cost $35.5 million in 1979, and that just filling out the required reports chewed up thirty-four employee years."

The *Journal* reported that a study made by "The Business Roundtable," a corporate executive group, indicated that "compliance costs for forty-eight major companies for 1977 showed that they laid out $2.6 billion over and above what good corporate citizens normally would have spent for environmental protection, employee health and safety, and other matters if the six government agencies hadn't intervened." The *Journal* indicated that some economists projected "that the extra cost for all business exceeded $100 billion."

Local Government

The implementation of the Air Quality Management Plan in Ventura California reached a ludicrous but calamitous extreme with the case of the Ventura Marina entrance. As a result of severe storms, the entrance to the Ventura Marina was clogged with sand and became unnavigable. The Port District, under pressure from over 1,000 harbor-locked boaters, fishing boats, and boat repair yard owners, finally obtained federal funds to dredge the entrance in early 1981. Their joy and relief was shortlived for they were notified by the Air Pollution Control District (APCD) that they could not dredge without an APCD permit. The rationale was that the dredge engine would generate emissions, and the Port District did not have an Air Quality Management Plan allocation from the APCD.

The Port District was in a "Catch 22" situation. Without an allocation, they could not get a permit and without a permit the Port District could not dredge. In the meantime, the boat repair yard was losing $41,000 per month. One sport fishing boat alone was losing $39,000 per month, and the recreational sailors were furious at being harbor-locked.

To solve the problem, the Port District was forced to seek "emission allocation donors" in order to borrow someone's unused emission allocation (if available) that they needed. If the emission problem could be solved, the district faced additional opposition from environmental interests. The protectionists were determined to stop the district from depositing the dredged sand on shore as they feared it might interfere with the spawning of grunnion. The California Coastal Commission, partially funded by federal funds, also threatened to sue the district if they didn't get a permit from them.

In the nation, as in Ventura, similar situations exist where federally mandated programs have resulted in local loss of traditional land-use planning and growth controls to federal and state agencies and their insensitive regulations.

Tellico Dam, Tennessee

In Tennessee, after five years of construction, work on the almost-completed Tellico Dam was halted for three additional years because the snail darter fish was declared an endangered species. The environmentalists thought the fish had only one natural habitat located in the Little Tennessee River, which would be harmed by the construction of the dam. During this interim period, the snail darters were transplanted to other rivers in the hope that they would reproduce elsewhere.

After Congress and President Carter exempted the project from the Endangered Species Act in September 1979, the $130 million dam was completed. On November 1, 1980, the *Los Angeles Times* reported that the snail darter fish had been discovered in another location in the South Chickamauga Creek in Chattanooga by an ichthyologist.

There are hundreds of similar cases illustrating abuses of power at the expense of citizens. This is an account of the taking—the taking of individual liberties, property holdings and local government autonomy, all in the name of preserving the environment.

Chapter Two

Save the Land

No single government program elicits such mass bipartisan support as the federal and state park systems. Their inherent lure of open space and recreational facilities for future generations has an almost universal appeal. However, few Americans know of the methods and extent of federal and state park acquisitions. The victims who *have* experienced the parks' acquisition methods hold an opposition to it that is real, adamant, and feverous. Vivid examples of this opposition are found in the revolt of the National Inholders Association, composed of landowners within federal park boundaries; the "Sagebrush Rebellion" of thirteen western states against federal domination of land holdings; the entrenched battle over the Alaska wilderness; and the increasing local government and citizen opposition to state and federal acquisition efforts.

The federal government's policy of acquiring more and more land represents a great change from the early days of our country. Originally, the United States had about 1.8 billion acres in wilderness and the federal government owned all of it. To raise money for the treasury, land was offered at $1.25 an acre in the 1830s and 1840s.[2] Even at those low prices, the government could not sell all the land. From 1862 to 1978, the U.S. granted 288 million acres, primarily to homesteaders. To encourage the railroad's expansion, about ninety-four million acres were given to the railroads. As an inducement to join the Union, an additional 328 million acres were granted to new states. To date, the federal government has sold or given away 1.1 billion acres of this original 1.8 billion acres, leaving about 775 million acres under federal control. The Defense Department holds about 33 million acres, the Department of Agriculture 189 million acres, and the Department of the Interior 548 million acres.

The National Park Land Grab

In August 1978, *Newsweek Magazine* focused on "Land Grab by Parks" and the instances of arrogant excesses by federal park officials. A directive had been issued by the National Park Service for federal park officials to eliminate through acquisition all private property holdings in or adjacent to federal parks within four years. Some of the property involved was owned by people who had lived their entire lives in the wilderness and in no way threatened or impaired the federal park program. There were some 36,000 of these "inholders," i.e., people owning land within or adjacent to a federal park. As the number of cases of land acquired from inholders mounted, a national pattern emerged of unrestrained harassment of American citizens by federal officials in Grand Teton National Park, Zion, Voyageurs, St. Croix, Cuyahoga Valley, Cape Cod, Fire Island, Blueridge Parkway, Buffalo River, and Wawona-Yosemite Parks, to name just a few.

The evidence was frightening: (1) Jim Downey, a 76-year-old mountain resident, was threatened with federal condemnation of his home if he proceeded with plans to add a bathroom to his cabin in Yosemite; (2) the residents of Wilsonia in King's Canyon National Park in California complained that federal, park-operated plows had deliberately pushed snow on top of older porches and rooftops in the community to force their collapse and then denied rebuilding permits; (3) the residents of Kelly, Wyoming, after petitioning for secession from the federal park, were landlocked when the park service deliberately stalled the clearing of a town access road following a 40-inch snowfall; and (4) an increasing number of communities within park boundaries were condemned by federal government, boarded up, and left to become ghost towns of former homes, shops, schools, and churches.

Iron Mountain Grill

To Pauline and Jay Dixon, the experience of the federal parks acquiring their land was very personal. The Dixons had opened the Iron Mountain Grill in 1934 and almost twenty years later built a nearby home in Mount Rogers, a rural area in the southwest corner of

Virginia, highlighted by the 5,700-foot mountain that bears its name. With the creation of the Mt. Rogers National Recreation Area in the 1960s, the Dixons' commercial and residential site was threatened with impending acquisition by the federal government for a scenic highway.

In late 1973, the Dixons were served with a "declaration of taking" and given twenty-one days to leave their home. After a number of years and a costly court trial the government finally acquired the grill, yet thereafter abandoned its plans and proceeded to rent the Iron Mountain Grill to the same person who had leased it from the Dixons. Today when they drive back, Pauline Dixon said, "I used to cry, but I don't look that way anymore."

The federal park program is very skillful in acquiring property at great pain and loss to the owners, only to later abandon whatever plans it had for the land, either letting it go unprotected and undeveloped or returning it to its former commercial use, but under government supervision.

Death Valley

In Death Valley, the federal parks used less subtle pressure than it did on the Dixons. Park rangers trespassed onto private property and drew shotguns to stop a man from mining his own property. Their justification was that the mining was incompatible with the adjoining federal park. However, incompatibility is not grounds for a government agent to invade private property and threaten the owner's life, all without legal proceedings and in blatant disregard of our judicial system.

The Inholders

In the summer of 1978, resentment of federal harassment came to a head. A husky, mountain man, the son of a federal park ranger and a resident of Yosemite National Park, set out across the country in his camper to meet with other landowners within federal parks. He hoped to share his experiences, hear theirs, and deliver a message.

Charles Cushman spoke of his fear that overzealous protectionists within the National Park Service perceived of a system in which their ends justified any means. He spoke of increasing harassment by park officials of residents in every federal park and federal land holding in the country. He described an apparent pattern and policy to eliminate private property holdings of people who had lived their entire lives in mountain areas and whose existence did not in any manner threaten or impair the federal park programs.

"We're the Indians of 1978," Cushman shouted to groups of inholders (landowners in or adjacent to federal parks), as he warned of the destruction of constitutional rights of 36,000 Americans and their land absorption into the 31-million-acre National Park System.

The admonitions of Cushman were echoed in the alarming testimony of United States Senator Ted Stevens of Alaska who stated in the Congressional Record on August 8, 1978: "For years we had a policy of land going out of federal ownership and out of public ownership. The federal government made land grants to the states; the states in turn made land grants to counties and local governments. The purpose of this process was to get land into private ownership in this country, to maintain a tax base, and to have a land ownership consistent with our free enterprise system."

Stevens described how the process seems now to have taken the reverse direction. He cited the hypocrisy with which federal authorities condemned the entire town of Kelly, Wyoming. Located within the Grand Teton National Park, the town of Kelly was condemned on the grounds that it was "incompatible" with park use; but, at the same time, park officials continued to maintain residential homes within the park for use by federal park authorities. Senator Stevens stated: "So now we have a double standard that if you live within a national park and you are a private citizen living on property that you owned prior to the establishment of the park, you are subject to condemnation. But if you work for the government or the park service, you can depend upon the use of taxpayer's funds to build a subdivision within the park for your private use." He continued, "I think it is time that we started a property owners' revolt as far as the exercise of this condemnation authority is concerned. It is arbitrary; it is capricious."

The revolution began, led in great part by the wandering Charles Cushman and his newly formed National Inholders Association, as 36,000 inholders resisted federal acquisition of their land and its absorption into the 31-million-acre National Park System.

The "Sagebrush Rebellion"

The "Sagebrush Rebellion" manifests the attitude of hostility held by the western states toward continuing federal domination and management of lands. The rebellion was launched in response to a series of federal actions designed to bypass state and local land management practices. In 1976, Congress passed the Federal Land Policy and Management Act, which declared that public lands would remain in federal control "in perpetuity." In 1978, President Carter invoked the Antiquities Act to "lock up" great portions of the state of Alaska. Also that year, the U.S. Forest Service submitted to the president recommendations for yet additional wilderness area designations. Finally, the federal government openly challenged the supremacy of state water laws.

To the residents of eastern and southern states, the actions of the federal government may not seem as alarming as to those in the West who are faced with massive federal land ownership and growing federal arrogance and disregard of local needs and feelings.

The Sagebrush Rebellion is a response to excessive federal land encroachments and controls by power bases in the eastern United States. To some, the threat represents a philosophical dichotomy between liberal-oriented sectors and conservative laissez faire attitudes of the American political process. To others, an economic motivation is apparent, as stated in the *Wall Street Journal:*

> This lock-up of public and private lands in the western states is a result of intense lobbying pressure, and we doubt that the public understands the consequences. The Independent Petroleum Association says that as a result of law or administrative procedures about 500 million federal acres, roughly one-fourth of the U.S., are off-limits to oil and gas development. At a time when we are growing increasingly dependent on unstable foreign sources of energy, the most rapidly growing aspect of the American economy is the land and resources that are being removed from development. . . .
>
> To bring undeveloped, privately owned western lands into development is now next to impossible, and to expand development in developing areas has been made more difficult. It is, after all, difficult to do anything when air and water must remain pristine.
>
> Whatever the intention, the result has been to hold down the economic development of the western states, thus protecting the eastern labor unions, industrial plants and resources from competition. . . .
>
> The environmental movement provides a convenient mask for any eastern legislators who want westerners for customers, not competitors.

Nevada kicked off the actual Sagebrush Rebellion in 1979 when its state legislature passed a bill asserting that the State of Nevada was the true owner of forty-nine million acres of land then under the control of the Bureau of Land Management (BLM). Several other states quickly joined this rebellion with similar legislation of their own.

The rebellion, however, is also a manifestation of the separate needs of individual western states. In Alaska the "Tundra Rebellion" struggles to enforce the federal promise, made when Alaska became a state, that 150 million acres of federal lands would be turned over to state control, while opposing federal acts that unreasonably restrict this land to one use only: wilderness.

Utah became the next state to join the rebellion when it passed State Senate Bill 5. Utah has since been led in this rebellion by Senator Orrin Hatch and become a home base of the League for the Advancement of States' Equal Rights (LASER).

Wyoming joined the rebellion when House Bill 6 was passed in the 1980 legislative session. The Wyoming legislation goes beyond Nevada's declaration of land ownership in that it not only claims ownership of the federal BLM lands but those lands of the United States Forest Service as well.

The State of Washington passed a rebellion bill when the 1980 legislative session went one step further than Wyoming and approved an amendment that removed from the Washington Constitution the disclaimer clause relating to unappropriated public lands. Washington, like many other states, had been coerced at the time of statehood into disclaiming any assertion over unappropriated federal public lands.

Even Hawaii joined the rebellion when it passed a resolution in 1980 that endorsed state control of public lands. New Mexico and Arizona followed suit, joining the rebellion in 1980.

Other states stand on the verge of joining the rebellion. They include California (which has authorized a study of the financial and legal results of public ownership after Governor Brown's veto of a rebel bill); Oregon (which will introduce rebel legislation in 1981); and Idaho (which directed its attorney general to study the possibility of supporting Nevada's legal challenge).

In the words of Nevada rancher Dean Rhoads, the Sagebrush Rebellion involves the "biggest land transaction on this continent since the Louisiana Purchase." Over 400 million acres are involved, which include many of the untapped oil and coal reserves of the United States, commercial forest land, and also the habitats of various endangered species.

On July 4, 1980, only days after Governor Reagan's campaign appearance in Salt Lake City when he proclaimed himself a "rebel," the citizens of Moab, Utah, staged a Fourth of July rally widely called the "first shot of Utah's Sagebrush Rebellion." It consisted of a bulldozer attack on a proposed wilderness study area of the federal government. By this act, a cheering crowd of Utah citizens disqualified the area from federal wilderness consideration and established their opposition to the federal control of lands.

The Sagebrush Rebellion continues, a backlash of western states and individuals against federal dominance and control and the preemption of local autonomy.

On August 3, 1979, Senator Orrin Hatch, joined by senatorial colleagues Goldwater, Cannon, Stevens, Helms, Garn, Zorinsky, de Concini, Jebsen, Simpson, Laxalt, and Wallop, introduced Senate Bill 1680, which provides for federally owned lands to be transferred to those state governments that have established State Land Commissions for control and maintenance.

The G A O Investigation

In response to the increasing criticisms of and challenges to National Park Service practices and the alarming extent of federal acquisition, the leading park proponent within the United States Congress, Congressman Phillip Burton, Chairman of the Subcommittee on National Parks and Insular Affairs of the House of Representatives, called for an investigation. The General Accounting Office (GAO) thereafter prepared a report of the private land acquisition policies and practices of the National Park Service, the Fish and Wildlife Service of the Department of the Interior, and the Forest Service of the Department of Agriculture, which repudiated the federal acquisition process.

On December 14, 1979 the GAO issued a report severely criticizing the federal government's policies and practices of purchasing land without first examining less expensive methods of protecting its environment. The report was equally critical of the unnecessary extent of federal land acquisitions throughout the United States by all three services. The report, entitled "The Federal Drive to Acquire Private Lands Should Be Reassessed," presents a comprehensive analysis of the conduct of the National Park Service, Forest Service, and Fish and Wildlife Service through an examination of various projects within the federal system and the recent land acquisition policies affecting each project.[3]

The GAO report found that the federal government owns more than 750 million acres of land[4] or approximately one-third of all the land in the United States. Over 90 percent of this federally owned land lies in thirteen western states. (See Figure 1.) The extent of federal ownership of property in the United States varies in each region from extensive ownership interest in western states (California, 44 percent; Nevada, 86 percent; Oregon, 52 percent; Alaska, 95 percent); to the range of ownership in midwestern states (Nebraska, 1.4 percent; Iowa, .6 percent); to the typical ownership interest in the eastern states (New York, 1 percent; Pennsylvania, 2 percent; Connecticut, 3 percent). Of this federal ownership, approximately 90 percent of the acreage is forest, wildlife refuges, or grazing areas; 3.5 percent is parks and historic sites; 3.5 percent is oil and gas reserves; and 2.4 percent is military bases.

Of great significance, the GAO report noted the extent of rapid expansion of federally owned land, the substantial associated costs, and the network of over 100 implementing administrative statutes governing the three investigated agencies. The fiscal basis for the growth has been the Land and Water Conservation Act of 1965. The act's goal is to assure "accessibility to all citizens . . . such quality and quantity of outdoor recreation resources as may be available and are necessary and desirable for individual active participation in such recreation."

In turn, the act established the Land and Water Conservation Fund, which provides funds for approved state and federal programs and is derived from four sources of federal revenue: surplus property disposals, motor boat fuel taxes, recreation fee receipts, and outer continental shelf mineral leasing receipts. By 1978 this fund had provided more than $1.6 billion to federal agencies and $1.9 billion to state agencies for implementing approved programs. The fund currently provides $900 million annually for grants to various programs. The National Park Service relies entirely on this fund for acquisition, while the Forest Service and Fish and Wildlife Service have even additional revenue sources.

Specifically, the report criticizes the practices of the three acquisition agencies for: (1) excessive and unnecessary expenditure of federal funds; (2) excessive and unnecessary acquisition of privately owned lands into federal ownership domain; and (3) failures of each agency to consider rational and viable alternatives to public ownership. These findings are based on thorough investigations and interviews and specific analyses of the implementation of various park projects throughout the park and wildlife systems of the three services.

The report concluded that "land acquisition practices followed by federal agencies result in some lands being purchased that are not needed. At many of the projects visited, the prime criteria for acquiring land appeared to be availability of funds and opportunity to purchase, rather than a critical determination of need. At other projects, the agency was buying everything within a project's boundaries, or as much land as the law allowed, without determining whether those lands were essential to achieve property objectives. In newly designated areas, agencies generally began acquiring lands as soon as funds were available and before land management plans or specific project objectives had been developed".[5] The GAO findings confirmed abuses echoed by Charles Cushman years earlier.

Land Acquisition Techniques

The federal and state governments acquire private property in two ways: by direct condemnation and payment of just compensation or by indirect acts, which confiscate property holdings without compensation. There exists an illusion among Americans that when a government files an eminent domain (condemnation) action to acquire a citizen's property, that citizen can be assured of being justly compensated in a fair and equitable manner. Yet the actual practice harbors a different reality, a reality of years-long court cases, costs, and government abuses designed to frustrate the constitutional guarantee of just compensation.

Under both state and federal law, an owner whose property is subjected to condemnation is entitled to just compensation based on the fair market value of the property for its highest and best use. Yet the road to that determination is often blocked by subtle government acts designed to devalue that use and value before a jury.

In recent years, federal and state government entities have attempted to devalue properties and to present to juries an appraisal or valuation that has little resemblance to the true value. This development has occurred because of bureaucratic attitudes, insufficient funds to acquire the property, and the realization by federal and state park proponents that their dreams for large parks and open space could not be accomplished with awards of fair market value. Many officials seek to achieve a low property value through a fictitious, and in

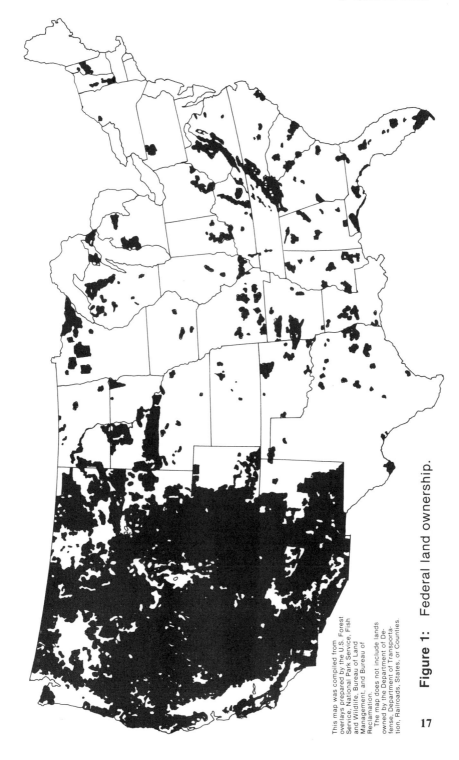

This map was compiled from overlays prepared by the U.S. Forest Service, National Park Service, Fish and Wildlife, Bureau of Land Management, and Bureau of Reclamation.

The map does not include lands owned by the Department of Defense, Department of Transportation, Railroads, States, or Counties.

Figure 1:   Federal land ownership.

17

reality fraudulent, underestimation of value (called in the trade "low-balling"). A sampling of the abuses follows below.

Convoy Lake National Wildlife Refuge

The Convoy Lake National Wildlife Refuge designated approximately 10,200 acres of land and water as a refuge for wildlife. It is a refuge established by the Migratory Bird Conservation Commission to preserve wildlife in Convoy Valley near Glenwood, Washington. Funds for this refuge are derived from the sale of duck stamps required of all waterfowl hunters.

As of October 1978, the Fish and Wildlife Service had acquired 6,700 acres, which had cost the federal government in excess of $1.1 million. The GAO investigation concluded that this was "an ill-conceived project, designed more to spend available acquisition funds than to meet program objectives." In fact, an earlier GAO issued in September of 1968 had questioned the very establishment of the Convoy Refuge on the grounds that of the 10,000 acres approved for acquisition only 144 contained water and marshes, and at least 4,000 acres in the refuge were biologically unessential to waterfowl habitat. Notwithstanding this prior warning, over the next ten years the Fish and Wildlife Service proceeded to acquire 6,700 of the 10,000 acres at the cost of $1.1 million, without even developing the Refuge to improve its potential as a wildlife habitat.

Nicolet National Forest

In 1928 Congress established the Nicolet National Forest, which encompassed 973,000 acres in the northern part of Wisconsin. The GAO commented that the Forest Service was in the practice of acquiring properties within the boundaries of this park without any determination as to whether or not the acquisitions would fulfill critical program or management needs. "Lands are purchased primarily on the basis on availability of willing sellers and acquisition funds rather than the satisfaction of critical project needs."

The examples given by the GAO include the acquisition of large lakefront tracts at a cost of $620,000 when the Forest Service already owned much of the lakefront area and had sufficient public access and camping facilities. The acquired properties had extensive improvements, including a summer residence and large recreation camp, both of which added to the cost of the property and will be destroyed by the Forest Service.

The San Francisco Bay National Wildlife Refuge

In 1972, Congress authorized the San Francisco Bay National Wildlife Refuge. This refuge comprises about 23,000 acres of marshes, mudflats, open waters, and salt ponds in the San Francisco Bay. To date the Fish and Wildlife has acquired through a "declaration of taking" over 15,000 acres of salt ponds previously owned by and leased back to Leslie Salt Company.

As one example of needless acquisition for the refuge, the service purchased five acres outside the initial refuge boundary to build a visitors' center. It chose as its site the former location of a boatworks. It could have shared space with a county marina, next to the boatworks, and created an excellent planned environmental educational center on land donated by the City of San Jose. Instead, the federal service acquired the boatworks land at a cost of $345,000 and spent an additional $573,000 relocating boats. The direct relocation costs, which were initially estimated at $132,000, have now exceeded $573,000.

These exorbitant sums were wasted on a site that was unnecessarily acquired since adjoining sites were available and could have been shared with other related civic facilities and programs.

Voyageurs National Park

In 1971, land along the northern United States border, east of International Falls, Minnesota, was designated the Voyageurs National Park. The purpose of this park was to preserve part of the route of the Voyageurs, a group of guides who were employed by early fur traders and who contributed significantly to the opening of the northwestern United States. The park encompasses about 220,000 acres of which 80,000 are under water.

GAO concluded that the National Park Service purchased all land within the project's boundaries without considering alternate acquisition methods. The Federal Park Service had adopted a priority classification for acquiring first, all lands that were developed or were considered to have high development potential; second, all isolated lands such as wilderness areas; and third, all other lands. Despite these priorities, the park proceeded to purchase any and all properties as soon as appraisals were completed, without regard to their priority. Thus, only 130 acres, or less than 1 percent of the entire park area, is actually in development zones to be used intensively (supposedly the first priority), and much of the park will remain accessible only by

19

foot, watercraft, or snowmobile (land of the lowest priority).

The GAO delineated the service's wasteful purchases:

1. A deteriorated hotel and ten acres with no road access costing nearly $200,000 that will continue to be operated by its original owner as a concession.
2. A 19-acre piece of property with a lodge and twelve cabins bought for $280,000, but which will also continue to operate as a concession.
3. A 23-acre island costing $118,000; because the original owner declined a concession on the island's lodge, cabins, and dock, the service will demolish the entire structure.
4. A fourth resort that was appraised at $185,000, a value that was contested by the owner and increased by a jury to $650,000, after which the Park Service decided it did not need the property and settled out of court with the owner for $500,000, leaving the owner a life estate.

Yosemite

In 1890 Congress set aside a parcel of land (eventually to become Yosemite National Park) located in the California Sierra Nevada Mountains and encompassing about 761,000 acres of property. As of July 1978, the government owned 759,000 acres or 99.8 percent of the planned parklands. The Park Service has been acquiring all privately owned land within the park boundaries as well as condemning lands to prevent uses that are incompatible with the park's purposes. The service proceeded with no acquisition priorities or use of alternative control strategies such as land-use restrictions.

One of the most controversial aspects of Park Service acquisitions has occurred within the Yosemite National Park, where over 172 separately and privately owned acres in the town of Wawona were designated for acquisition in order to eliminate, in the words of the agency, a class of "special privilege" persons who have homes inside a national park. This action by the National Park Service engendered tremendous antagonism from local residents. Charles Cushman stated: "If Wawona were a jumble of apartments and fast food joints, then I could see the [Park Service's] point, but this town has been here longer than the park itself, and it's hurting no one."

The Case of Big Sur, California

Barely had the ink dried on the indictment of the federal land policies by the GAO, when the National Park Service, led by United States Senator Alan Cranston and Congressman Phil Burton, began a federal "land grab" of Big Sur, California.

It would be extremely difficult to capture in words the majesty of Big Sur, the rugged majestic mountains, forests, and steep bluffs perched above the Pacific Ocean. It is a community of artists and farmers, the very rich and poor, and ranchers as well. The breathtaking majesty and extraordinary character of this community is without parallel.

On April 24, 1980 United States Senator Alan Cranston addressed the Senate Energy and Natural Resources Committee on Parks to support his Senate Bill 2551 for acquisition of property holdings within Big Sur. "The rights of homeowners must be safeguarded, so should the rights of all Americans and all posterity, to enjoy the fantastic stretch of undeveloped coastline—the longest and most scenic in the contiguous forty-eight states . . . those who know and love Big Sur want to preserve it the way it is today. This is especially true of the residents of the immediate area."

With those words, Senator Cranston placed in motion the vast acquisition machine of the federal government by which 48 miles of Big Sur coastline in Monterey County and San Luis Obispo County, including over 120,000 acres of privately owned properties and 578,000 acres of government-owned land would fall under the jurisdiction of the United States Forest Service.

Was this community and 48-mile-long coast threatened by rampant development? Was there a threat of environmental deterioration of Big Sur that required the involvement of the federal government?

Historically, Big Sur has been precluded from any substantial development, real or threatened, by several constraints. First, Big Sur can never be over-developed due to the ruggedness of the mountains, lack of access, unavailability of water and sewage treatment facilities and potential geological instability. Second, the residents of the area have traditionally resisted large-scale development efforts and cooperated with local county zoning restrictions while land use has been severely constrained by the California Coastal Commission. All of these constraints have prevented any noticeable development in Big Sur. Although the proponents of the Park Service were the first to cite the potential drain upon water, sewer, and highway systems by continued development, the facts reveal that only eighty-eight homes have

21

been approved for construction along the 48-mile coast in the last eight years (an average of eleven per year). Nevertheless, the federal government, encouraged by environmentalists and "no growthers," proceeded to develop a plan for federal control, acquisition, and regulation of the Big Sur Coast.

In addition to Cranston's bill, federal control was encouraged by the Big Sur community's congressional representative, Leon Panetta, who introduced a version for federal control of Big Sur in the United States Congress different from Cranston's.

Panetta stated, "There is really no question but that this remarkable and unique area must be preserved . . . there is no disagreement among the residents or visitors to this: they want Big Sur to stay the way it is and so do we all. We all recognize that there are forces at play at the present time which make preservation of Big Sur difficult to achieve. There is increasing development of homes and residents."

The plan had been set in motion: a federally controlled scenic area of almost 700,000 acres, purchased by the park system through an appropriation of an estimated $100 million.

Responding to possible federal control initiatives, Big Sur residents met in an overflowing Grange Hall to hear Charles Cushman. "What is happening in Big Sur," Cushman declared, "has happened many times elsewhere, and it usually ends up with creating a national park; and what usually happens is that the individual rights . . . the human rights . . . are taken away."

Cushman warned the outraged group that the promises of the federal government that their lands would not be acquired, their homes would not be acquired, nor people be relocated were not reflective of the history of the National Park Service. He stated that "presently there are 21,000 condemnation lawsuits in federal courts . . . during the last fifteen years 65,000 families have lost their land."

He compared the promises of the federal government in Cuyahoga Valley (between Cleveland and Akron, Ohio) with the fact that an original estimate of $34.5 million park legislation proposing removals of only twenty families escalated to the acquisition of 550 homes, the removal of 300 families and acquisitions amounting to over $100 million. He continued, "The old buildings and landmarks have been torn down, burned down, and boarded up. Promises made today will be changed later."

The citizens' opposition to federalization of Big Sur was spearheaded by Gary Koeppel, publisher and editor of the Big Sur

Gazette. For over two years, Koeppel dedicated his personal assets and professional life to inform the local residents of the plans for federal control or acquisition of the Big Sur coast. The gazette became the only source of disclosure of the government's plans, and the rallying source for opposition. In April 1981, the gazette published its final edition to commemorate the failure of federal plans.

The first hearing of the Cranston bill was supported by a combination of environmental groups, including the Big Sur Foundation, the Sierra Club, and the Wilderness Society, all of whom supported the act as a means of averting development pressures. A remarkable event would transpire. Representatives of virtually 95 percent of the residents of Big Sur appeared through spokesmen in the senate hearings and decried the federal involvement as an unnecessary interference with local control, stating it was unnecessary for any environmental consideration and would, in effect, turn the Big Sur coastline into a federally sponsored Coney Island.

The hypocrisy of the bill was reflected in its estimates for capital acquisition and its alleged motivations. The Cranston bill called for a ten-year acquisition program of approximately 125,000 acres of privately owned lands at a cost of $100 million. This appropriation belied reality. In the public testimony of the president of the Big Sur Chamber of Commerce, Mr. Don A. McQueen: "Most acreage within the 125,000 acres designated for public acquisition is selling for minimum prices greatly in excess of the estimates of the federal government, which alone would result in an acquisition cost of $725 million rather than $100 million represented by Senator Cranston." Mr. Howard Sitton, another resident of Big Sur, stated: "Nothing in the bill speaks about the costs of condemnation or maintaining such a project. It would be more realistic to think in terms of hundreds of millions of dollars rather than the estimate of Senator Cranston."

Senator Cranston advised the United States Senate that the Big Sur project would not, as compared to other prior federal projects, result in the needless forced condemnation of private property holdings. He stated, "Generally, I contemplate land acquisition on a willing buyer, willing seller basis. I have written into the legislation strict controls on the use of condemnation. To repeat, there will be no use of condemnation except under the very limited circumstances specifically mentioned in the bill."

Senator Cranston concluded that condemnation would occur only if the Secretary of Agriculture found that the property of the owner had undergone a change in use that was incompatible to federal park projects and, even then, the secretary could not acquire more than 5 percent of the total private lands necessary for public access and recreational use.

The apparently reassuring statements of Senator Cranston concerning federal acquisition practices had unfortunately been made many times in the past, only to be disregarded by the bureaucrats. Time and time again, as with the Indians in the 1800s and early 1900s, the federal government was not true to its word. The following cases verify this fact.

The St. Croix National River Project began on August 8, 1967 when Senator Gaylord Nelson stated to Congress, "We intended the secretary's powers of condemnation to be used to protect scenic and wild rivers from commercial and industrial destruction, not for indiscriminate acquisitions. This bill is not a land grab and the condemnation power is primarily for acquisition of appropriate public access and sites." In response to then-Senator Mondale's inquiry whether the bill would require purchase of fee interest of the land, Senator Nelson responded that "the only acquisition of homes and property may be within the access points themselves." Today nearly every home within 400 feet of the river has been purchased.

In 1966 the Indiana Dunes National Lakeshore exempted various communities from condemnation and specifically guaranteed no condemnation. In 1976 the law was amended to allow condemnation. Soon thereafter, two-thirds of the town of Beverly Shores was taken out of the exempt status. The 1978 legislation proposed to take the rest of Beverly Shores and within six years acquire the balance of the community, including 330 homes, schools, shopping areas, churches, and gas stations.

In Yosemite National Park, inholders were protected by a number of statements by members of Congress who guaranteed "all valid and existing rights," but numerous condemnations and restrictions *have* taken place.

In Cuyahoga Valley National Recreation Area the law specifically limited acquisition except for specific administrative needs and to protect the resources. By July 1978, over 300 families had been forced to sell under threat of condemnation. What followed included the destruction of small farming communities and mass relocation of an entire population and culture.

In Big Cypress National Preserve acquisition was limited to those deemed absolutely necessary. Initially, 46,000 landowners and 1,000 pieces of property were protected from condemnation. Today, less than 100 of those improved properties are protected and almost all the remaining lands have been acquired through purchase or condemnation.

Against this background Senator Cranston stated that lands would not be acquired in Big Sur unless absolutely necessary and that the funds appropriated for acquisition would be used only where all other means had failed. Is he to be believed?

The Cranston Bill did not receive sufficient support in the United States Senate subcommittee, for countless landowners protested in defense of their own constitutional rights. However, Congressman Leon Panetta introduced a bill that went even further than Senator Cranston's in guaranteeing that no condemnation would take place and that a combination of local citizenry and a federal control panel would be established to create a land-use plan for the entire area. However, his plan duplicated the California Coastal Commission's planning activities, which had been in progress for seven years.

The efforts to acquire Big Sur by the federal government had been supported in the United States Senate by Michael Fischer, California Coastal Commission Executive Director, who indicated that the California Coastal Commission supported a federal project in Big Sur. In fact, at that time there had never been a public meeting, public hearing, evidence, testimony, or a vote by the Coastal Commission concerning Big Sur. Moreover, Fischer, in a letter to Congressman Leon Panetta dated April 17, 1980, stated: "A series of studies by state and local government agencies confirms that only limited capacity remains in Highway 1 [the main road along the Pacific Ocean in California] and that projections for recreational demand indicated doubling within twenty to twenty-five years. . . . Highway capacity for visitors will exist only if we accept highly congested traffic conditions with an average traffic speed of thirty miles per hour or less."

Despite this statement and background as to the traffic conditions and impact upon Big Sur of potential development, the Coastal Commission through Michael Fischer and Congressman Leon Panetta, and sponsored by the park chief, Congressman Phil Burton, demanded a federal park control system, which by all estimates would increase the visitors to Big Sur from an annual total of three million per year to *over twelve million per year*. Since the park proponents suggested a bus transportation system starting from outside the boundaries of the park, gigantic parking facilities for hundreds of thousands of cars would have to be established at both ends of the park. With this influx of federal visitors, a tremendous demand would be put on existing food, lodging, fuel, water, and sanitation services.

25

The same "environmentalists" who subjected landowners to years of administrative battles, hearings, environmental impact reports over one building home site along the 48-mile coast now loudly supported a huge federal park with an additional nine million visitors per year and the potential devastation of the environment, air, water, and traffic without question and without an environmental impact study—a case of "loving the area to death."

In July 1980, the Panetta congressional bill, which promised no acquisition of private property, but rather a combination local citizenry and federal control for the development of a master plan for Big Sur, was introduced. It went before Congressman Phil Burton's subcommittee and passed two minutes after its announcement. The next day, the Interior Committee of the House of Representatives passed the bill in fifteen minutes, but added an amendment—the allocation of $35 million *for the acquisition of private property holdings.* Finally, to this amended bill were added excessive powers of moratorium to the effect that if the federal government designates a property for acquisition, its use and development can be *banned permanently,* all without hearings, evidence, or compensation. Can our federally elected officials be trusted?

Santa Monica Mountains National Recreational Area

On November 10, 1978, President Carter signed into law the Santa Monica Mountains National Recreation Area (SMMNRA), assigning to the National Park Service the responsibility for preserving the mountains' natural, cultural, and recreational value. The SMMNRA encompasses approximately 150,000 acres in an area of Southern California ranging 47 miles across from Griffith Park to Point Mugu State Park, and averaging 7 miles in width. The park is bounded by the Pacific Ocean on the south, the San Fernando Valley-Thousand Oaks area on the north, the Oxnard urban area on the west, and the Los Angeles urban complex on the east.

Upon a visit to Agoura Valley (about 20 miles northwest of Los Angeles), a central clog of access to this project area, which is hot (100° in summer), dusty, dry, and surrounded by high, almost inaccessible mountain ranges, one asks, "Why pay for this?" The Santa Monica area already includes four state parks (Point Mugu, Malibu Creek, Topanga, and Leo Carillo), public reservoirs, military installations, and school grounds; there are plans for additional state land acquisitions for public use, and the area is governed in great part by the land controls of the California Coastal Commission.

Within six months of the enactment of the SMMNRA, the familiar scenario of the Federal Park Service had resurfaced: how to acquire such massive acreage with insufficient funds—only $155 million. On May 30, 1979, Congressman Anthony Beilenson requested the intervention of local governments to "preserve" the lands until they could be federally acquired. In cooperation with the Sierra Club, Beilenson asked for a series of comprehensive acts to block landowners from the subdividing of land, grading, and building and to oppose the extension of roads, water lines, and public works projects that would service the properties. In October 1979, the Sierra Club formally requested that the Los Angeles County Board of Supervisors adopt an interim moratorium. That request was rejected by the Board of Supervisors, in great part because it would result in a taking of property without payment of just compensation and thus violate the U.S. Constitution and the Federal Civil Rights Act.

There have been massive expenditures for properties (with little if any public recreation potential), delays, and agency collaboration in down-zoning and restrictions of land-use. Smaller landowners have been left to dangle and have been denied use of their property, without payment of compensation. All of this has occurred, not to provide a park for national use, but to preserve the character of the mountains and permit the use by some local Los Angeles citizens.

The Alaska Wilderness Bill

President Carter declared the Alaskan Wilderness Bill to be "the conservation decision of the century." In the 1958 Statehood Act, which established Alaska as the forty-ninth state, Congress promised to give title to Alaska of over one-third of the state from "vacant, unappropriated, unreserved" federal land. With passage of the Alaskan Bill in 1980, the state finally got title to 150 million acres. In 1958 all but one percent of Alaska's 377 million acres was owned by the U.S. government. A condition to its statehood involved the return of 150 million acres to local control.

Since the 1958 federal commitment to return lands to Alaska's ownership, a number of extreme environmental pressure tactics have derailed the rights of Alaskan citizens. First, the Prudhoe Bay pipeline, a natural economic asset, was successfully blocked for ten years because of concern over its impact on caribou migrations (a concern that turned out to be unjustified). Riding on the success of this disruption victory, environmentalists turned to the cause of wilderness designation and insisted that most of Alaska be maintained as a wildlife refuge.

A number of recent measures have even further reduced Alaska's chances of collecting on its promise from the federal government. In November 1978 the Secretary of the Interior withdrew from consideration 110 million acres of land for management by the Bureau of Land Management. In December 1978 President Carter imposed a 1906 Antiquities Act designating 56 million acres as national monuments and ordered the immediate study of an additional 30 million acres for possible inclusion in the National Wildlife Refuge System. In 1980 the Alaska Wilderness Act designated over 104.3 million additional acres of prime virgin forest, magnificent mountains, and prospective oilfields as virtually untouchable wilderness preserve. As a "wilderness area" the lands are off limits for timber harvesting and exploration for mineral and oil extractions.

The U.S. Geological Survey estimates that federal land, much of it in Alaska, contains 40 percent of the nation's undiscovered oil, 47 percent of the undiscovered natural gas and 40 percent of the total coal reserve. In addition, it is recognized that sixteen of the eighteen minerals considered vital to national security are found in Alaska; however, the Alaska Wilderness Act in great part precludes their exploration.

Thus, as our nation becomes increasingly dependent upon foreign oil and tension escalates in the Middle East, our Alaska still suffers breach of its statehood covenant and is denied use of its land, which could otherwise help alleviate our energy problem. And all of this because of environmentalists who, in the words of the Los Angeles *Herald Examiner,* "have the time, money, and stamina to facilitate excursions an average tourist cannot afford."

California's Land Acquisition Program

The environmental movement to "save the land" has witnessed extraordinary acts by the federal government in the acquisition and management of land. Acts that are often contrary to statehood compacts and individual and states' rights and are usurpations of the concept of private property. Yet this movement has been encouraged by simultaneous activities of state and local governments. Most indicative of this effort is the State of California.

In California, the land acquisition process traditionally has been used to purchase property necessary for highway construction and streets (by the Department of Transportation) and land for recreational purposes (public parks and beaches maintained by the Department of Parks and Recreation). The latter acquisition is

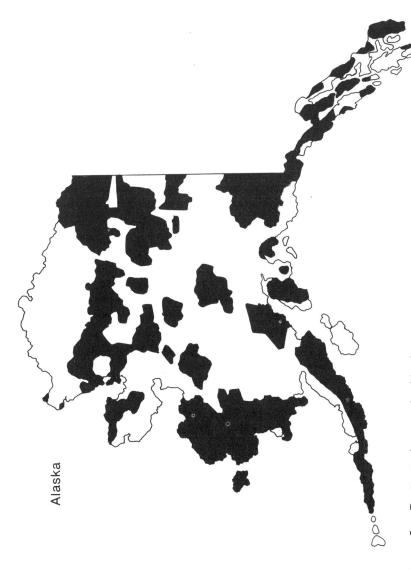

Alaska

Figure 2: Protected areas in Alaska.

planned and managed by the Department of Parks and Recreation with approval given by the Public Works Board of the State of California. Parks are funded through one of two methods: direct legislative appropriations for a specific acquisition of private property or, more recently, major statewide bond issues that identify and plan acquisition of various designated properties.

The planned acquisition of properties by the Parks and Recreation Department is based on two acquisition lists, one that is available and disclosed to the public and another that is confidential and of questionable secrecy. The first list, named the "Five-year Capital Outlay Program," combines a series of land acquisitions that are financed during a five-year period by available funding.

The second list is an overall plan for acquisition of properties throughout the State of California. It is not available to the public and appears on monthly updated computer run-out sheets entitled "California State Park System Acquisition Priorities." It divides various properties into three potential acquisition categories: "Natural Heritage Preservation," "Cultural Heritage Preservation," and "Outdoor Recreation." The secret computer list was inadvertently disclosed in superior court proceedings in San Mateo County in March 1979 in the case *"Loftus, Power, and Law* v. *the State of California."* At that time, the manager of the Parks and Recreation Department testified to the existence of the computer list and his understanding that the computer list was not available to the public, including elected representatives.

This latter revelation forebodes substantial danger to landowners throughout California. Not only does the secrecy of this planning method pose a dangerous threat to a democratic society, but more immediately, it is unfair to landowners who are spending money and time to develop and use their property, without the knowledge that various agencies are planning to acquire it.

In California, the creation of the Coastal Commission added another factor to the state land acquisition process. The Coastal Commission engaged in acquisition activities without either the funding or authority to implement the planned acquisition. California's acquisition program for parks and beaches is restricted to the recommendations and planning of the Department of Parks and Recreation and to the funding approved through the Public Works Board on the basis of money made available by the state legislature or bonded enactments.

However, an inordinate amount of staff time of the Coastal

Commission was expended to create their own list of possible acquisitions of private property holdings, in spite of the fact that the Department of Parks and Recreation was the only government agency created and funded for that purpose.

This development had a detrimental impact on property holdings throughout California. A "behind-the-scenes" policy has been followed by the commission: permits for the development and use of land that was on the Coastal Commission's "hit list" were systematically denied. This occurred despite the fact that the Coastal Commission had neither funding, legal authority, nor assurances that the property in question would ever be acquired.

At the time that drafts of proposed Coastal Commission acquisitions were submitted for public hearings, the staff of the commission was given guidelines and policies by the state to deny projects that were contrary to the public use anticipated by acquisition. This policy resulted in projects (whether a simple extension of a deck on a house, the construction of a home, or the completion of a major community project) being precluded from development on the basis of the Coastal Commission's acquisition list.

The particular application of this Coastal Commission policy in California soon created a possible violation of constitutional rights. On one hand, landowners were historically guaranteed payment of just compensation for the acquisition of their properties and yet on the other hand they were denied use and development of their properties on the basis of a possible acquisition that was neither funded nor approved. The "Catch 22" situation found a number of owners in major disputes with California public officials, the Coastal Commission, and the Department of Parks and Recreation in an attempt to bring their property out of the limbo, non-use, and non-development, and non-payment by the state.

Wolfback Ridge: A Case Study of Government Collusion

The Lynch case of Wolfback Ridge in the town of Sausalito, California, represents a problem of far greater complexity than previously described cases. The case arose from the implementation of the "Golden Gate National Recreational Area," which reflects more than any other national park project the growing, subtle conspiracy and cooperation among federal, state, and local governments and environmental groups to achieve public use of private property through unfair and inequitable valuation practices.

The Golden Gate National Recreation Area (GGNRA) was introduced to the legislature by Congressman Phil Burton in June 1971, a culmination of the goals of avid conservationists to protect many of the undeveloped scenic resources of Marin County, which is the northern link of the famed San Francisco Golden Gateway. The creation of the GGNRA reflected a number of years of combined community activities of federal and local officials, various citizens' advisory groups and environmental organizations.

One of the largest proposed (and eventual) land acquisitions of the GGNRA was a 156-acre parcel along a mountain ridge within the City of Sausalito known as Wolfback Ridge. It commands some of the most magnificent scenic vistas in the San Francisco Bay. This land holding was owned by three families (FitzSimmons, Lynch, and Melchoir) who soon became victims of the bureaucracy.

Advised of the federal activities to acquire their property, the owners of Wolfback Ridge commenced development applications for residential use of their property. It very quickly became apparent that local officials reviewing the applications were participating in the acquisition plans of the federal government. By July 1971 the owners had already been denied development applications by the City of Sausalito. During this period, the city informed Congressman Burton of its support of the GGNRA and its willingness to take action necessary to insure its passage of the GGNRA in Congress. The city feared that if Wolfback Ridge were developed it would establish higher market prices that would affect the ability of the federal government to acquire the adjoining properties.

In November 1971 the City Council of Sausalito denied the owners' third application for development, based on "planning considerations." Within a month, the city communicated with various congressional representatives as to the danger of land sales and development that could increase land values and hence federal acquisition costs. In 1972 the owners submitted and received rejections of a fourth and then a fifth development application, while the city officials of Sausalito were in communication with the United States Congress and Department of the Interior to assure the acquisition of Wolfback Ridge. In addition, the City of Sausalito retained a lobbyist from Washington, D.C. to further support the inclusion of Wolfback Ridge within GGNRA and provided testimony before a national parks subcommittee of the necessity for its acquisition.

By October of 1972, the city was advised by its GGNRA lobbyists of the necessity for additional time but was concerned about its ability to continue to "hold off the owners." Finally, by April of 1973, one of the assistant administrators of the GGNRA advised the senate committee that the potential costs for its acquisition of Wolfback Ridge could range from $250,000 to $8 million, with the owners making it clear they would not accept less than $25,000 per acre for a total of approximately $4 million. Nevertheless, environmentalists (without any expertise in acquisition costs) represented to the United States Congress that the property could be obtained for a fair market price in the range of $260,000! At the same time, the mayor of Sausalito advised the senate subcommittee that Wolfback Ridge could be acquired for no more than $250,000!

Throughout 1974, the City of Sausalito submitted to the National Park Service the status of various development plans by property owners in the Wolfback Ridge area. The park service in turn advised local annexation agencies of its hope that "there would be no development on the property which would destroy its future acquisition by the NPS (National Park Service)." In July 1974 the Sausalito city council denied the owners' sixth application for development (a subdivision of 311 homes on 156 acres), and within six months Wolfback Ridge was finally added as an acquisition target for the GGNRA in a bill signed by President Ford.

It became apparent that the City of Sausalito could not continue to hold off the owners from development, and in May of 1975 the city adopted an outright moratorium banning any development of the properties within the GGNRA for a minimum of one year.

After having "toyed" with the property owners through six applications and over a period of five years, the City of Sausalito finally declared an outright denial of development for any use at all.

In September 1975 the federal government offered the Wolfback Ridge owners $1 million for their property. Meanwhile, the federal government also installed a wire fence barrier virtually blocking access to the property and had the terrain patrolled despite the fact it neither owned nor had paid for the property.

On July 12, 1976, five years after the introduction of GGNRA and after the owners' five post-park development application denials, the United States filed a condemnation action to acquire the Wolfback Ridge property. Despite the fact that the government had already offered the owners $1 million for their property, the government's testimony as to the value of that property was reduced to $300,000—only $300,000 for 156 prime residential acres overlooking the San Francisco Bay, acres that were actually worth in the range of $4 million.

In June 1977 the owners prevailed in federal court with a jury award of approximately $3.8 million. Again, the federal government initiated delay by deliberately appealing this decision with the knowledge that the appeal could delay payment for the property for an additional three years to one owner in particular who was already dying of cancer and needed the money immediately. After extensive arguments, the appeal was dropped and the "just compensation" became available to the Wolfback Ridge owners in December 1978. Unfortunately, Frank Lynch, one of the owners, had died of cancer a year earlier.

The "games" played by Sausalito are not unique in California. A large number of cities use similar tactics in cooperation with federal and state agencies to achieve land-use or growth goals.

In the case of the planned Santa Monica Recreational Area of Southern California, federal officials were advised[6] to encourage local citizens and residents in the Santa Monica Recreational Area to participate with Los Angeles County and related local governments to achieve a temporary freeze on land-use and development pending completion of the proposed Santa Monica federal park. The federal government was encouraged to lull the citizenry into enacting local restrictions on their own property under the assurance that those restrictions would never be used to alter or influence the value of their property in a court determination of value. In effect, they were told to "trust us."

The advice was the same for the residents of Big Sur who were subjected to congressional plans for a federal park. The local citizenry were advised by officials to "cooperate" and restrict the use of their property as a temporary and yet necessary measure prior to land acquisition by the government, and that those restrictions would never be used to cheat the landowners out of their property's true value. The words of a staff memo to the director of the National Park Service, William Whelan, dated January 8, 1980, were specific: "They should further state that in any subsequent land acquisition by NPS (National Park Service) the appraisals will disregard any lowering of property values that results from the zoning procedure. Once local property owners recognize that they will not be economically harmed in any subsequent NPS land acquisition, they may be more receptive to NPS zoning suggestions."

Yet within the same memorandum of the National Park Service, a different and contrary directive would go to federally retained appraisers and establish the basis of their subsequent valuation of the citizen's property. That direction was clear and explicit:

> Direction to appraisers: consult with the solicitors' office to determine which zoning assumption should be made. As a general interim rule, *NPS involvement in pre-park creation zoning should not invalidate using the resulting zoning for fair market appraisal purposes.* (Italics are the authors'.)

Thus, after telling landowners that they would not be financially injured by park-induced restrictive zoning, the National Park Service directed its appraisers to the contrary, that they were to use the NPS-induced zoning in their appraisals.

The federal and state acquisition process continues, often unabated and funded by limitless tax revenues—all under the guise of "saving the land."

Chapter Three

Save the Coast

In January 1980, numerous California citizens journeyed from various coastal communities along California's 1,000-mile coastline to vent their anger to federal officials over the conduct of federal and state coastal management practices.

Over two consecutive days, the federal Office of Coastal Zone Management conducted hearings in Los Angeles and San Francisco and received overwhelming evidence of radical, illegal government conduct. This evidence was submitted by a broad range of society: agriculture, labor, real estate, landowners, utility and energy companies, and an enraged citizenry. The federal authorities refused to tape record or transcribe the hearing testimony, for it was an accounting of government bureaucratic abuses without parallel in American history: stories of the tragic loss of Betha Lankovska; the endless struggles to salvage John Steinbeck's Cannery Row; the altered federal map of Inglenook Fen; the missing tapes of the Clayton application. Victim after victim argued for the cessation of federal funding, the fiscal cut-off of the Coastal Zone Management Plan.

In the name of "saving the coast," radical bureaucrats, without restraint or accountability, had built their own system of dictatorial policy. Extortion, misrepresentations, abuse of constitutional rights and social engineering followed as the natural aftermath.

The Coastal Zone Management Act

The continental shoreline of the United States (excluding Alaska and Hawaii) extends over 53,000 miles and constitutes one of our country's most valuable natural resources. Our coast supports commerce, recreation, fishing, housing, and agriculture. The nation's seven largest cities, 53 percent of the population, and 90 percent of recent population growth occurred along our coastlines.

In the 1960s, concern for potential deterioration of the coast generated a demand for more extensive government regulation of our coastal uses. To help protect the coastlines, Congress passed the Coastal Zone Management Act (CZMA) in 1972, and offered incentives in the form of federal loans and grants to state and local governments for coastal zone planning and management.

The objectives of the act were to provide economic development consistent with appropriate environmental protection. Congress stated in its Declaration of Policy for the Coastal Zone Management Act: "It is the national policy...b) to encourage and assist the states to exercise effectively their responsibilities in the coastal zone through the development and implementation of management programs to achieve wise use of the land and water resources in the coastal zone, giving full consideration to ecological, cultural, historic, and aesthetic values, as well as to the needs for economic development. . . ."

The major goals of the CZMA were to: (1) protect the nation's unique and significant natural resources; (2) protect historic and cultural resources and provide for increased recreational access; (3) manage rapid and widespread coastal development; and (4) coordinate and streamline federal and state decisions affecting coastal resources.

Thirty-five coastal states and territories were eligible to receive federal funding under the planning phase of CZMA. Between 1974 and September 1979, $70 million was distributed to various states to enable them to develop coastal management programs.[7] Fifteen of the eligible states have received federal approval for their coastal management plans, and to date are now receiving second stage, implementation grants on a cost-sharing basis. The overwhelming majority of the eligible states (thirty-one out of thirty-five) have developed new regulations designed to increase protection for the use of coastal resources.

Perhaps the most dynamic and certainly the most far-reaching coastal management program was the one developed in California.

The California Coastal Commission

The climate, topography, and land use varies widely along the California coastline: sandy beaches, sand dunes, rocky cliffs, housing projects, artichoke fields, and foggy redwood forests all are present. The countless pockets of vacant, undeveloped beach lands in the northern part of the state contrast sharply with pockets of concentrated development in such areas as Malibu and Redondo Beach in Southern California. While some sections of the population enjoy easy public access to the beaches, other frustrated residents struggle through limited beach access and scant parking accommodations.

In keeping with the Coastal Zone Management Act emerged the rallying cry, "Save the Coast" by the proponents of Proposition 20, the 1972 California initiative that created an organization known as the California Coastal Zone Conservation Commission. California soon became both pathfinder in trends in environmental coastal management regulation and precursor of national events. There can be little doubt that this initiative was spawned in great part by instances of unrestrained and avaricious development of property along parts of California's 1,072-mile coastline. The 1972 California election centered around Proposition 20 and the Pacific coast. A propaganda war began between its supporters and opponents. The proponents cited instances of an industrial rape of the coast, which threatened wall-to-wall development akin to a Waikiki or Miami Beach. Opponents warned of further loss of individual rights due to yet additional government regulation.

The political campaign focused upon the apparent failure of some local governments and the elective process to regulate the desires of landowners and developers alike, as some developments proceeded unrestrained and with little concern for aesthetics or the public's need and right to use and enjoy the coast.

In November 1972, the California electorate adopted Proposition 20 and created the California Coastal Zone Conservation Commission (later renamed California Coastal Commission) with the understanding that it would be a temporary organization. During its four years of existence, the commission was to prepare a master plan for development and use of the coast.

Proposition 20 created one statewide commission and six regional commissions[8] which in the words of the first chairman of the Coastal Commission, Melvin Lane, were created to "prepare a plan for the future of the California coast, and to regulate coastal development temporarily, while the plan was being prepared."

Each regional commission was responsible for the preparation of appropriate plans,[9] while simultaneously administering a permit process that proceeded in the interim—a process to insure that unwise development did not transpire before the completion of the plan.

In essence, a new layer of government had been created to administer control over the use of all land located within the specifically defined "coastal zone."

Proposition 20 created a two-part coastal zone: a "planning area," which extended to a maximum of five miles inland[10] and a "permit area," which extended 1,000 yards inland from the mean high-tide line of the sea. The coastal zone permit area covered a total of 545,000 acres.[11] For all properties within the permit zone, formal approval by the regional commission, and in some cases the state commission, was necessary for the owner to proceed with any development or alteration of his property, whether that proposal be for a hotel, a house, a fence, or even brush removal. The only exception to this permit requirement was through an exemption, which a property owner or developer could gain by proving that he had a vested right to development as a result of substantial expenditures prior to November 1972. There was also an appeals process in which permit decisions by the commission could be contested.

It was this exemption and the abuse of the appeals process by the commission that would lead to so many of the grievances against it.

The findings and declarations of policy of Proposition 20 contained a plethora of generalities that provided a poor guide as to the substantive implementation. Proposition 20 declared:

> The People of the State of California hereby find and declare that the California Coastal Zone is a distinct and natural resource *belonging to all the people* and existing as a delicately balanced ecosystem; that the permanent protection of the remaining natural and scenic resources of the Coastal Zone is a paramount concern to present and future residents of the State and nation; that in order to promote the public safety, health, welfare, and to protect public and private property, wildlife, marine fisheries and other ocean resources in the natural environment, it is necessary to preserve the ecological balance of the Coastal Zone and prevent its further deterioration and destruction; that it is the policy of the State to preserve, protect and, where possible, to restore the resources of the Coastal Zone for the enjoyment of the current and succeeding generations.[12] (Italics are the authors'.)

Within the Coastal Act, an appeals procedure was established to insure uniform application of the Coastal Act policies and to provide administrative relief to those dissatisfied with the decision of the regional commissions.

When a regional commission voted to deny a permit, the applicant could appeal the decision to the state commission. By the same process, a permit that had been *approved* could be appealed by *any* organization or member of the public who opposed it. However, the public could not appeal a regional commission permit denial. Finally, the state commission could not hold a hearing on an appealed application unless a "substantive state issue"[13] was raised. If the commission found there was no substantive issue, then there would be no hearing on the project's merits by the state commission, and the decision of the regional commission would stand.

This permit process soon became one of the most controversial aspects of the California Coastal Commission's management program. From 1973 through December 1979, over 40,000 applications for projects were processed by the regional commissions, with the majority processed administratively without the necessity of the full public hearings. But applicants with hearings found themselves subjected to a new set of rules and regulations, unfamiliar to a democratic system.

Upon receiving an application for a development permit a regional commission prepared a "Staff Report—Project Summary" concerning the development. Certain minor developments that had little or no potential adverse impact on coastal resources could be acted upon administratively by the executive director of a regional commission or be placed on the regional commission's "consent calendar." Permits that could have a potentially substantial impact on the environment or coastal resources were subjected to full public hearings before the regional commission and their appointed commissioners. Although these constituted a minority of the total permits processed by regional commissions, they reflected the overwhelming majority of projects having any consequential impact.[14]

On the basis of the vague and inclusive statements of purpose in Proposition 20, staff reports soon challenged every conceivable "fault" with proposed projects as justification for their denial. Architectural design, soil stability, water and sewer availability, type of use, location, and access were just a few of the innumerable grounds for attack by the commission. This myriad of reasons for recommended denial presented a roadblock to approval, *regardless* of whether the landowner already had approval for each separate item from his locally elected government.

To respond to a permit denial, which often included extensive staff summary reports and dozens of reasons, an applicant was allocated a brief and in most instances inadequate time to rebut the challenges. Five and ten-minute hearings became routine. In addition, the hearings were open to third parties, who, regardless of their interest in a project, could make additional protests to its approval and were often given the same time period as the applicant himself. Furthermore, an applicant shared equal rostrum time with the local representative of the Sierra Club or a similar environmental group.

Time restrictions severely curtailed an applicant's legal rights, because any subsequent challenge to the commission's decision in court was limited by state law to the "administrative record," i.e., what had transpired during the course of the hearing, and excluded any evidence that had not initially been heard by the commission. Thus an applicant could be denied the opportunity to present his full case due to a time limit and then barred from presenting his complete case in future court hearings.

There was yet still another stumbling block in the permit process. A regional commission's approval of a permit could be appealed to the state commission by any "aggrieved person." The Coastal Act identified an "aggrieved person" as someone who, in person or through a representative, simply *appeared* at a public hearing of the state or regional commission, local government, or port governing body in connection with the case. This recklessly broad provision allowed any "environmentalist" to simply attend a hearing and object, however so briefly, to a permit, thereby initiating an automatic appeal against an applicant whose permit had previously been approved by the commission. This appeal would frustrate and delay the entire project since approval then had to be sought from an additional tier of government.[15] (See Figure 3 for an overview of the complexity of the permit process.)

This appellate practice resulted in numerous abuses as frivolous appeals flourished. Of the appeals taken to the State Coastal Commission,[16] 55 percent were initiated by individuals or organizations other than the applicant. Most of those appeals were filed by the Sierra Club, Coast Watch, and other organizations concerned with stopping or regulating *any* development along the coast that they disapproved.

In addition to these unfair appeals practices, the commission adopted a unique concept of majority rule. From 1973 until 1978, the bylaws of the state commission required that a project be approved by

COASTAL DEVELOPMENT PERMITS IN THE CALIFORNIA COASTAL ZONE

by

JAMES A. FAWCETT
COASTAL PLANNING SPECIALIST
UNIVERSITY OF SOUTHERN CALIFORNIA
SEA GRANT MARINE ADVISORY SERVICES

and

BARBARA A. KATZ
AREA MARINE ADVISOR
UNIVERSITY OF CALIFORNIA
SEA GRANT MARINE ADVISORY PROGRAM

AUGUST 1979

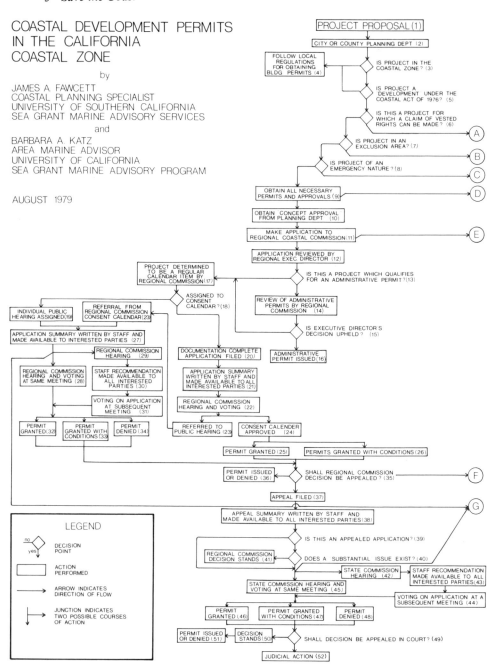

Figure 3:   Development permit process in the California coastal zone.

a majority vote of the *total* commission, *not just a quorum* (which is the standard requirement for most organizations, including Congress). Absent commissioners were automatically considered as votes against a proposed development permit. Because all members of the commission were rarely present at one time and because vacancies existed through non-appointments, just a few "no" votes often would be sufficient to deny a permit, even though the majority present actually voted in favor of it. This arrangement made it very difficult for any project opposed by even just a few preservationists to receive approval.

California's Coastal Plan

In accordance with the Coastal Act of 1972, a coastal plan was prepared at the end of 1975 and submitted by the Coastal Commission to the California State Legislature for approval. The coastal plan consisted of a 443-page plan with 162 suggested policies within the nine required categories. There were also forty-four recommendations for action by government bodies concerning the plan. After much debate and disagreement within the state legislature due to opposition of the plan by cities and counties affected, the legislature *disapproved* the plan.

This placed the environmental interests and supporters of the Coastal Plan in a dilemma. When they could not get the Coastal Commission plan adopted, supporters of the commission persuaded the state legislature to include most of the policies of the plan in a new Coastal Act of 1976.

In late 1976, the California legislature gave the commission a second chance to devise an acceptable coastal plan and extended the life of the Coastal Commission in order for them to complete their work. The authority of the regional commissions was extended to oversee a new coastal plan (local coastal programs) to be completed by June 1981. The State Coastal Commission was extended indefinitely. This temporary state commission became permanent with adoption of the Coastal Act of 1976.

By virtue of the Coastal Act of 1976, each of the fifteen counties and fifty-three cities affected by the Coastal Commission were required to submit a Local Coastal Program (LCP) for approval by the Coastal Commission. The local programs were to be consistent with the policies of the Coastal Act, and after review and approval by the Coastal Commission, the LCP becomes the city's or county's program for coastal conservation and development.[17] After their approval and implementation, the LCPs regulate all applications for development along the coast, and the regional commissions are to expire.

Throughout its life (1973 through publication of this book), the Coastal Commission has increased its size, the number of its regulations, and its funding. Whereas Proposition 20 stated the purpose and guidelines of the Coastal Act in three and one-half pages, the Coastal Act of 1976 is a document consisting of eighty pages and seven articles. The California Administrative Code (entitled "Title XIV, Natural Resources, Division 5.5, California Coastal Commission") consists of 132 pages of fine print explaining the rules and regulations of the commission. In addition, each regional commission developed interpretive guidelines to explain what was meant by the policies within the Coastal Act of 1976. By the end of 1979, the guidelines consisted of 159 pages of explanation.

The original appropriation of $5.5 million for the four-year life of the 1972 commission expanded beyond recognition. The funding went from a total of $376,416 in the first year (1972) to a forty-three fold increase in 1980–81, making a total of $16,441,216 (est.) in expenditures during that fiscal year. The total amount expended by the State Coastal Commission from 1972 through 1980 exceeded $57,674,073. (See Figure 4 for a summary of the Commission's appropriations from 1972 through 1981). The commission staff grew from approximately fifty in 1972 to 210 in 1981.

The Federal Coastal Zone Management Act, and hence federal taxpayers, funded the Coastal Commission staff and commission operations in an estimated $12,675,021 from the fiscal year 1977 through June of 1980. The Federal Coastal Energy Impact Program funded the commission with $4,236,653 through the same period. The Federal Estuary Sanctuary Planning Fund provided an additional $20,440 for an estimated total of $16,932,114. Another $1,153,771 was received by the State Coastal Commission from the Liquified Natural Gas (LNG) Terminal Act. There has been additional indirect support by federal agencies. The American taxpayer subsidized the California Coastal Commission's program and management of the coast at a combined cost in excess of $57 million.[18] And it continues.

Abuse, Excess, and Bureaucratic Bungling

The procedural guidelines that governed the permit and exemption process perhaps more than anything else encouraged the coastal com-

Figure 4: California State Coastal Commission budget appropriations.

Budget Year	General Fund*	Bagley Conservation Fund**	Federal	Total
1972–73	$ —	$ 376,416	$ —	$ 376,416
1973–74	302,735	2,130,863	—	2,433,598
1974–75	549,324	1,902,134	1,074,762	3,526,220
1975–76	1,018,930	1,389,461	1,117,288	3,525,679
1976–77	3,152,735	728,471	927,950	4,809,156
1977–78	6,418,595		2,504,887	8,923,482
1978–79	5,547,255		2,291,861	7,839,116
1979–80	6,191,898		3,607,292	9,799,190
1980–81 (est.)	7,059,371		9,381,845	16,441,216
Subtotal	$30,240,843	$6,527,345	$20,905,885	$57,674,073
1981–82 (proposed)	5,547,255		4,150,000	11,051,993
Total	$35,788,098		$25,055,885	$68,726,066

*Includes reimbursements from other state agencies
**Includes fee revenue

mission's excesses. The five- and ten-minute hearings, the voting procedure, and the lack of opportunity for an applicant to respond fully to staff summaries and attacks on his proposed development, all served to evolve a system of unique rules and procedures with little, if any, restriction. Moreover, when the procedures became the accepted norm in the administration of the Coastal Act, the undemocratic abuses that followed were its natural offspring.

Although government excesses and instances of bureaucratic shams are common to most large state and federal agencies, the abuses that transpired in the name of the environment under the California Coastal Commission reached an extent without comparison both because of their extraordinary nature and the commission's widespread effect on several different elements of the population. The instances of excess affected low, moderate, and affluent income ranges, community associations, labor and business, agriculture, and local government itself, all financed at enormous taxpayer expense.

Public View Corridors

The Coastal Act was designed to provide, as much as possible, public access to the California shoreline. In addition, the act was adopted largely to prevent mass building projects and developments from obstructing public views of the ocean and access to the shoreline along various sections of the coast. In response, an immediate concern in the initial days of the Coastal Act was over attempts by developers to build large complexes that would deny potential access to the beach or substantially interfere with view slots along highway corridors of California's coastline.

Staff reports often dwelled upon whether a proposed development would substantially block views of the public toward the beach and ocean.

Proposition 20 and the Coastal Act of 1976 were not created to be blanket moratoriums on all development, and initially, the commission balanced various factors in order to determine the extent a proposed development could eliminate potential threats to view slot corridors. This balance was often achieved by a relocation of the proposed building or a diminution in its mass and size so as to avoid *substantial* interferences with the view slot. In other instances, buildings were allowed to remain within the view slot, but with the condition that appropriate aesthetic considerations be included, such as the addition of vegetation, color, and architectural design.

Gradually, as the power of the commission grew, handling of potential view slot obstruction expanded from one of balancing all of the factors involved in a project to an automatic grounds for denial of the project. Thus an environmental consideration initially designed to moderate development became the basis for an overt moratorium on all development. The case of Victoria Consiglio is perhaps the best example of how a relatively worthy and simple guideline was excessively enforced by the commission, without regard for individual justice or property rights.

The Case of Victoria Consiglio

Victoria Consiglio purchased a two-acre parcel of land located on "Kasler's Point" in southern Monterey County along the Big Sur corridor overlooking the Pacific Ocean. Her acquisition, typical of American ownership, was based on an initial diminutive down payment with indebtedness secured by first deed of trust. The property is located in the middle of a residential enclave extending approximately 1-1/4 miles along the Big Sur Coast and surrounded by residential development on eighteen of twenty-seven residential parcels.

Her parcel is perched on a steep cliff with treacherous access to the rocky shore below and located substantially below a public vista point along Highway 1. In 1978 Victoria applied for and received a permit from the County of Monterey to build a modest one-bedroom home of approximately 1,000 square feet. It was to be situated on the parcel in such a way as to minimize all visability of it from Highway 1. The permit included provisions for replanting natural vegetation and cypress trees along graded areas to further screen the house from public view.

In April 1979, Victoria applied to the Central Coast Regional Commission of the State Coastal Commission for approval of the home. Victoria received a 7-6 affirmative vote; but, the permit was refused. Why? Because it was ruled that *three absent members* of the commission deprived her of a majority.[19]

In essence, the denial was based not on whether the proposed house would block a view of the ocean, but instead on the mere fact that the house and its access road could be seen at all by the public. In this instance, the only manner in which the public could see the house was to lean over a vista point railing, look straight down to a bluff below, and envision the roof of the house which would be built. No

47

view to the ocean was blocked; no access to the beach was blocked; the proposed house was denied simply because, once built, it could be seen.

To Victoria Consiglio, an immigrant from Germany, the sudden loss of her life savings by the arbitrary conduct of a government agency was inconceivable. "I believe that what's happening to me now can't happen under this Constitution. Nobody believes me when I tell them what's happened to me. . . . They say it can't happen. Well, it did."

Public Coastal Access

Another principal concern of Proposition 20 and the Coastal Act of 1976 was that the public have access to the coastline and that new developments not prevent that access. Future eyesores of a coast lined with apartments like those in Malibu or Oceanside were to be averted.

There were two major problems accompanying this environmental constraint. First, both the United States Constitution and California Constitution require that private property may not be taken for public use without payment of just compensation. The Coastal Commission, therefore, was to compensate landowners for providing public access to the shore. Second, there was difficulty in determining the necessity for public access among new developments that were proposed for the California coastline.

These environmental criteria were soon subjected to extreme administrative abuses by an overzealous staff, which allowed environmental dictate to exceed all standards of rationality. In October 1978, a number of homeowners in Malibu, California, sustained great personal catastrophe when a fire devastated a number of homes along the Pacific Ocean. Within a day of that catastrophe, the staff of the Coastal Commission announced that the homeowners would not be allowed to rebuild their homes unless they first agreed to *give* public access trails to the state without compensation. The commission dropped its demand in response to political pressure, including an environmentalist, Governor Brown, who referred to them as "bureaucratic thugs."

Agriculture Preservation

Preservation of valuable and viable agricultural lands on the state coastline was a high-priority item in the Coastal Act. In furtherance of this goal, the Coastal Commission established agriculture as a "priority use" of privately owned coastal land. However, in its zeal and enthusiasm, the Coastal Commission often attempted to "preserve" agriculture in cases where land was no longer suitable for agriculture due to poor soil, bad location, uneconomical size, or proximity to urban areas.

In San Mateo County, the southern neighbor of San Francisco, 90,000 acres of land were declared to be "prime agricultural land" by the commission. On the basis of this designation, landowners were restricted to nonfeasible uses (one dwelling unit per 160 acres). Agricultural soils in San Mateo County are depleted, subjected to the whims of nature, and economically marginal at best. Yet the priority of "agriculture" gave the commission an opportunity to down-zone, and ban residential and commercial development.

In some cases, the hypocrisy of the Coastal Commission and its policies was blatant. In the Muzzi and Clayton cases the stated policy of preserving agriculture as a "priority use" of coastal land was deliberately abandoned in order to frustrate the landowners and lower their property values so that they could be acquired more easily by the government.

The Muzzi Case

Domenic Muzzi was the elderly head of the Muzzi family, Italian land-holders who had extensive property holdings on the coastside of San Mateo County. Domenic, in the latter years of his life, wanted to revive the agricultural use of a 132-acre parcel called the "Pescadero Marsh."

Two years earlier, Domenic had farmed artichokes on the property but abandoned his efforts because of wetland flooding. Thereafter, Domenic spent a considerable amount of money in reclaiming the land and making it once again suitable for planting. When he proceeded with his plans to plant artichokes, he was challenged by a California Deputy Attorney General assigned to the Coastal Commission who said he would need a permit. In effect, agricultural planting was subjected to the same bureaucratic delays as a housing project. After many frustrating months, Domenic finally abandoned his attempts to farm the parcel. His reclamation—and the money spent on it—had been wasted.

The reasons behind this interference by the Coastal Commission with Domenic's artichoke field were not then apparent. Unbeknownst to Domenic, his property had for a long time been on a State of California acquisition list for use as a park. A couple of years after defeating Domenic's farming plans, the State of California initiated an eminent domain action to acquire the Pescadero Marsh as a public domain. However, the state appraiser contended that the property was unsuitable for agriculture (artichokes) and offered Domenic only one-fifth of Domenic's opinion of the property's value. Only then did it dawn on Domenic that his attempt to farm his property had been interfered with by the Coastal Commission in an attempt to "set it up" for public acquisition.

For four years, as a result of collaboration between state agencies, Domenic was prevented from both the use of his property and any compensation for its true value. In early 1979, after extensive negotiations, the State of California proposed and Domenic accepted a settlement offer, and the property was conveyed to the State of California. Unfortunately, Domenic died the night before the check arrived.

The Clayton Case

Mary Clayton, the 65-year-old co-owner of an oceanside ranch in California, which is bordered on the west by the Pacific Ocean, experienced frustrations quite similar to Domenic's. The Clayton family ranch, which consists of approximately 440 acres, had been consistently dedicated to agricultural use, despite the fact that in recent years agriculture was no longer economical and the land was much better suited to a low-scale residential development. However, in spite of the shortcomings, the Clayton family had maintained the agricultural use.

In late 1977, Mary Clayton sought to divide a 60-acre section of her ranch that was west of Highway 1 and located along a 1 1/2-mile stretch of the Pacific Ocean. This division sought to break off a 2 1/2-acre section of the property for a minor commercial use that could realize additional revenue in order to help support the farming on the balance of the property.

The Coastal Commission denied Mary Clayton's application, saying that the property division would increase the value of the property and thus increase the cost of its acquisition by the State of California, which was contemplating purchase of the entire ranch for public use.

Mary Clayton immediately protested. She insisted that her

property could not be frozen for the purpose of artificially restricting its value for eventual acquisition by the state. When she pointed out that statements to that effect violated her constitutional rights, members of the commission voted to remove the contents of the commission's statements from the public minutes. A number of days thereafter, Mary returned and borrowed the public tape recordings, only to find that the relevant statements on the tape had been erased.

Protection of Plant and Animal Life

One of the strongest goals of the environmental movement is the protection of endangered plant and wildlife. As in other matters, the commission's method exceeded all sense of reason.

Inglenook Fen

A fen is normally defined as "a vestige [indication] of special life forms based on the combination of two water sources in a watershed area." Approximately five miles northeast of Fort Bragg, California, lies an area known as Inglenook Fen. To the officials of California's Department of Parks and Recreation and the California Coastal Commission, this fen was reportedly of special historic significance, a 4,000- to 6,000-year-old relic of the Ice Age that supported twenty to twenty-five endangered plant and animal life forms.

On the basis of a study prepared by the state, which established the historic significance of the fen, the Coastal Commission imposed a set of moratoriums blocking development of over 1,000 potential homesites for the landowners in this Mendocino County area.

Soon thereafter, residents of the area began the long and arduous task of studying and comparing notes with the various scientific advisors who had been retained by the State of California to determine the historic significance of the fen. That study soon revealed that the "special and endangered species" living in the fen and identified by the government were not native, were not unique to Northern California, were not endangered, and in some instances were mislabeled or entirely non-existent. Of greater significance was the discovery that the state's case for the fen was based in part upon an 1874 map prepared by the federal government. Further research disclosed that this map, which described various surrounding physical characteristics of the adjoining properties, had been altered and that some of the map's symbols had not been invented until after 1874.

Had the state agencies bothered to do their homework and interview local residents and older generations of property owners they would have learned that, far from being a landmark Ice Age relic, Inglenook Fen was a fifty to sixty-year-old cattle watering hole, and nothing more. Instead, an altered map was allowed to be the primary basis for a moratorium on the building of homes.

The Lankovska Case

In the summer of 1978, Betka Lankovska applied for fire insurance for her home in Bera Canyon at Malibu, California. Because of heavy brush behind her home, two fire insurance companies confirmed that she would need to clear out the brush before a policy would be issued. To comply with the insurance companies, Betka requested permission from the Coastal Commission to remove brush on three to five acres and plant a family orchard of ten fruit trees on a portion of the cleared land. After filing the required paperwork during the first week in June 1978, she learned the papers had been misplaced by the Coastal Commission staff and so she refiled.

On September 22, 1978, Betka wrote to the Coastal Commission: "For almost two months I have been waiting patiently to hear from the commission that will allow me to bulldoze a firebreak in brush on some three to five acres of my land. This past week, we've had four fires in our area. This firebreak should have been in two months ago. If we lose our house, trees, and chaparral because you have caused this long delay, I will take necessary steps to compensate me for your neglect. This is an A1-1 area, high fire risk, and nothing will be harmed by clearing for fruit trees, grain, and necessary firebreak. Why do I need a hearing for something that would have happened naturally in an A1-1 area? I cannot wait much longer."

On October 12 (four months after the application had been filed) a Coastal Commission public hearing was held at which a representative of the Sierra Club objected to the issuance of a clearing permit until the property could be searched for an alleged endangered plant, *Pentachaeta lyonii,* which was *thought* to live in the area of Zuma Canyon. The plant is little more than a weed and is distinguishable from other more common plants in the area only by a botanist. After a number of phone calls to the commission staff office in an attempt to speed up the permit, Betka was warned by a commission staffer, "If you remove one bush from your property, you would or could be fined $10,000 or imprisoned."

On October 26, the Coastal Commission confirmed approval of the application. However, "prior to the issuance of the permit, the applicant shall submit a written agreement to utilize drip irrigation and temporary erosion control methods at the site for the brushing and shall have the method for accomplishing this approved and, if possible, supervised by the Topanga Los Virgenes Soil Conservation District." The drip irrigation system would have cost several thousands of dollars for a mere ten fruit trees.

However, the permit was at that point a moot issue, for on October 23, 1978, Betka Lankovska's house, outbuildings, and their contents were totally destroyed by the Agoura-Malibu fire. Of course, Betka Lankovska had no insurance, for without the all-important Coastal Commission permit to clear the land of dangerous brush it was unobtainable. Betka Lankovska, a divorced, middle-aged woman with two children, is legally blind, can work only two days a week, and must live on a limited income. In closing remarks to the federal panel that had assembled in 1980 to review the conduct of the Coastal Commission,[20] she said, "I ask that what happened to me should never happen again to a private property owner and that the Coastal Commission not have the power over a person's destiny as they did with me when common sense could have been used."

The Restoration of Cannery Row

A major objection to the Coastal Commission has been its involvement in local community affairs. This intrusion into local government planning has created bitterness and in some instances economic disasters, as the commission's "environmental protections" competed with overwhelming local, public, and commercial needs.

The impact of Coastal Commission decisions upon local government autonomy is reflected in its most tragic form by the case of Cannery Row in Monterey, California. Once the heart of a flourishing fishing industry, and the famous setting of several novels by John Steinbeck, Cannery Row now stands virtually vacant, a deteriorated rubble along the beautiful Monterey Bay in California.

For many years, until the 1950s, a booming sardine industry stimulated this area with 25,000 seasonal jobs and netted over 750,000 tons of sardines a year. In the 1950s, the sardines didn't return, perhaps due to excessive fishing and a disregard for ecological warning signs. The mile-long row of cannery buildings and wharves became a dormant remnant of that past, as the industry was gradually replaced by deteriorated piers, dilapidated buildings, gaping foundation, weeds, and debris.

But soon after its demise, the citizens and local government leaders of the City of Monterey began a vast new plan for Cannery Row that would mean a rebirth of the area into a commercial recreation center not unlike Fisherman's Wharf or Ghirardelli Square in San Francisco. The dream was to build a tourist attraction that blended the historic landmarks of the past with the bay-oriented commercial enterprise of the future.

In 1962, the citizens of Monterey developed and approved a master plan for Cannery Row. A decade later, in 1973, the plan was revised to accommodate commercial needs to the growing concern for protection of the coastline and historic sites. The 1973 master plan, drafted with the unanimous support of community leaders, civic groups, business, labor, and government officials, was for an integrated development of hotels, restaurants, and shops that anticipated over $23 million in construction and possibly over 3,000 jobs, which would amount to an additional 10 percent of the entire workforce of the City of Monterey.

From this 1973 revised master plan for Cannery Row came a number of plans to restore the buildings, maintain historic facilities, and slowly transform the site into one of the most beautiful tourist attractions in California.

One owner, Dale Runyan, planned to restore deteriorated old buildings in a historic area between John Steinbeck's "Doc Pickett's Lab" and the Hovden Cannery Building. The buildings originally contained approximately 71,000 square feet of floor area. However, they had been damaged by the elements to such an extent that the City of Monterey had declared them a public nuisance and issued a condemnation order. Runyan was directed to rehabilitate or destroy the structures, at a minimum cost of $70,000. As a result, Runyan conceived a development plan for rehabilitating the structures, preserving the historic Cannery Row facade and much of its structural character, and reducing the building area to approximately 51,000 square feet (42,000 square feet of commercial area and 9,000 square feet of public plaza).

The regional coastal commission recommended approval of the project, *but attached numerous conditions,* the most important of which was the size and scope of the buildings, parking accommodations, and water availability. In particular, the commission's staff suggested reducing the net leasable floor space from over 40,000 square feet to just 27,200 square feet and creating two new public restrooms at the two public entrances to the building.

This provision for new restrooms is of special interest because it effectively involved a scheme by which the project would be denied as a result of water constraints. The complication of adding restrooms was due to a water use limit on the development of 1,360 gallons of water per day: the public restrooms would consume an unforeseeable amount of water. In addition, the owner would be required every six months to submit written reports to the executive director of the regional coastal commission concerning the amount of water used in gallons per day during the preceding six months.

The *Monterey Peninsula Herald* referred to the whole affair as "the Cannery Row latrine," pointing out the extremes of the Central Coast Commission and "its bubble-headed staff" and the extent to which the commission will go to "undermine the fundamental purposes and intent of the California Coastal Conservation Act." "Its latest bungling of a project to convert some delapidated structures of Cannery Row into a useful and attractive commercial center in keeping with the area's tourist orientation boggles the mind. . . ."

The point here is that water management was actually under local government control and involved the Public Utilities Commission of California. Yet the Coastal Commission took upon itself this question of water constraints, effectively precluding the use and development of this part of Cannery Row and its conversion from debris to a commercial benefit to the entire community.

The largest development planned for Cannery Row was to be a hotel financed by a combination of investors led by the late Ben Swig, a hotel entrepreneur from San Francisco. The Swig Hotel was to have been built at the entrance to Cannery Row and would have been a 176-room, first class, luxury hotel overlooking Monterey Bay and Monterey harbor. However, in March 1978, a report from the staff of the Central Coast Regional Commission designated the entire site as a parking lot for skindivers.

Stan Harless, an investor and contractor for the site, echoed the hopelessness of the situation and, in speaking of the Coastal Commission said, "You're already hung when you come in. All they decide is what size rope they're going to use. It's like being led to the guillotine." The hotel site still sits in rubble, debris, and nonuse, pending a final determination by the Coastal Commission. In the interim, the rising costs of construction and the forced disinterest of investors raises the serious possibility that this public facility will never be built on Cannery Row.

Another project, the proposed Cannery Row Inn, met a similar fate. Mrs. Dorothy Long planned to convert an existing building that she owned at the entrance of Cannery Row into a thirty-two room inn. Mrs. Long received unanimous approvals from the City Planning Commission, Architectural Review Committee, Site Planning Committee, the building inspector of Monterey, and even from the regional coastal commission. But delays in groundbreaking resulted in a reappraisal and reversal by the Coastal Commission in 1976. The site remains undeveloped, and Mrs. Long has lost $50,000 of her life's savings earned as a school teacher.

The Spindrift Hotel, a historic building on Cannery Row, was condemned by the City of Monterey because its deteriorating condition along the ocean had made it extremely dangerous. Mr. Ted Richter acquired the site for $500,000 and spent over $40,000 in plans for rehabilitating the hotel and turning it into a European country-style inn of forty-two rooms, thus preserving an historic landmark in Cannery Row, providing access to the beach, private parking, improved views of the ocean, and additional jobs. Like Dorothy Long's hotel, this proposal has been held up by the Coastal Commission. During planning stages, when Richter revealed his plans to the staff of the commission, he explained the necessity of raising the roof three additional feet in order to properly renovate the top floor. The commission told him that such a dramatic change would cast an additional shadow into the bay waters and potentially harm underwater sea life. Another worthy project that would benefit thousands of people every year ''bit the dust'' over an unjustified commission whim.

One of the finest restaurants in Monterey is The Sardine Factory. It is located approximately two blocks up from the bay front of Cannery Row and, like its neighbors in Cannery Row, has been a target of the Coastal Commission's wrath. A few years ago, the restaurant owners desired to expand the banquet facilities and provide additional parking for its customers by removing a triplex apartment building that was on the property and owned by the restaurant. The triplex had been for the most part unoccupied and was quite dilapidated and run down. The Coastal Commission would not allow the property improvement because they said that it would eliminate low-income housing accommodations. They required that the owners devise a plan to relocate the triplex somewhere else in Monterey or, in lieu of this, agree to pay $15,000 into a subsidy fund for nonprofit or public housing development for lower or moderate income families in Monterey. Low-cost housing is a concern of local government and appropriate federal and state agencies. It is not a concern of an environmental commission. The Coastal Commission's actions had no relationship whatsoever to the protection of the environment.

Today, Cannery Row sits practically vacant and in ruins, the worst example of deterioration and the worst eyesore on the California coastline. Mayor Gerald Fry of Monterey testified to a California Senate subcommittee hearing in 1977 that the buildings were firetraps and that "if nothing is done, they'll all fall down." If the Coastal Commission had allowed the City of Monterey to complete its plan, Cannery Row would have tremendous potential for use and enjoyment by the public, the very public that the Coastal Commission pretends to advocate!

"The people are hurting," stated Frank Crispo, president of the Cannery Row Merchants' Association. "Without hotel rooms, there is no one on the streets during the day. The people who run the shops can hardly pay their rent. I tell them to hang on." This magnificent bay vista remains abandoned in rubble and debris, nurtured only by a few who still dream of its future: a tourist attraction and aesthetic restoration of historic sites, hotels, and restaurants with $40 million of construction and 3,000 jobs presently stalled. "I walk this street every day with tourists," Crispo commented, "and explain the history of what happened to us. 'Doesn't anybody care?' the tourists respond, and leave shaking their heads in disbelief."

Those on the commission who want to "save the coast" of John Steinbeck should listen to Mr. Steinbeck's own suggestion for improving Cannery Row, spoken to the *Monterey Peninsula Herald* in 1957:

> I'd like to see the whole place torn down and turned into something pleasant looking. . . . The coastline would be perfectly lovely once you got the fish scales out of it and put up some pleasant-looking places . . . Young and fearless and creative architects are evolving in America. I suggest that these creators be allowed to look at the lovely coastline and to design something new in the world, but something that will add to the exciting beauty rather than cancel it out.

Just as Baltimore permitted an imaginative developer, James Rouse, to improve sections of its delapidated waterfront (see Harborplace Photographs 14–16), Cannery Row (Photographs 8–13) could have been improved years ago, had the Coastal Commission not interfered.

Greenmail

Examples of excesses by the Coastal Commission are more than surpassed by countless instances of "greenmail," a euphemism for blackmail committed by government in the name of the environment. It is instances of the "greenmail" of private landholders that stimulate the greatest emotion and wrath at the way the Coastal Act has been implemented. This "greenmail" extortion has resulted in conveyances of large land holdings and financial donations to the State of California, the Coastal Commission, or one of its affiliated state agencies or departments.

Bailey and the Rocks

For days, the residents along Mussel Shoals, including Robert Bailey and his wife Caroline, watched nervously as the surf pounded closer to their beachfront homes. The high winds, unusually high tides, and strong waves were threatening to erode sand under their houses and damage the structures. During the low tide periods, Bailey and his neighbors paid a contractor to put 180 tons of rocks in front of their homes. It cost them $4,500.

Having survived the storm threat, Mr. Bailey's problems began anew. He was told he needed a county and coastal permit and that he made a mistake putting the rocks in without one.

Although the executive director of the South Central Regional Coastal Commission could have given Bailey an emergency permit over the telephone, his permit application was instead put on the consent agenda of the regional commission. At the meeting, representatives of the environmental group Coastwatch challenged the permit and asked for a full hearing.

Five months and many hearings later, it was decided by the commissioners that Bailey should dedicate his entire beach, right up to the rocks, to the public—to get a permit for work already done!

In conjunction with adjacent owners, Bailey and his wife decided to fight in court against this extortion of their property rights by the commission. They, like so many others, had voted for Proposition 20 not knowing it would turn into a bureaucratic quagmire. Bailey said, "We do not object to the public using the beach. The public roams freely. What we object to is the Coastal Commission coming in, demanding our property and demanding we give up property for a worthless piece of paper [permit]. It's illegal. It's unreasonable, and I resent it to hell."[21]

The Allen Funt Case

For Allen Funt, famed producer of the television show "Candid Camera," the matter was not funny. Allen Funt purchased a 1,200-acre holding in the Big Sur area of Monterey as a future retirement site. He envisioned a four-building enclave nestled high above the mountains and far from public view: a dwelling structure, a foreman's house, a small visitors' guesthouse, and a barn and stable. Those four structures constituted the entire planned development on 1,200 acres.

In discussions with the commission staff over his proposed project, Allen Funt offered to convey a 300-acre easement to the State of California for park purposes. Funt would have obtained some tax benefits with the gift. Not content with this voluntary offer, the Coastal Commission demanded much more.

The Coastal Commission first demanded an additional 270-acre scenic easement. This demand was later withdrawn, but the original, voluntary 300-acre easement was made a mandatory condition, thus depriving Funt of the tax consequence of his generous offer. Further, the commission required a permanent, recorded agreement by Funt not to subdivide the property, thereby preventing forever the sale of any piece of the property. (They also eliminated two of the four buildings in the plan and ordered that the remaining two buildings be constructed so that the lights could *never* be seen by the public at night.) Extortion? In the words of Funt's attorney: "Just another way of skinning the cat." And it was just that—only the "cat" was Mr. Funt and his personal property.

The Marina Dunes Case

In 1971 the State of California planned to acquire 22 acres of a 50-acre site for a freeway across the beach property of four investors in Marina City, California. Aware that the road would cut off access to the developers' remaining twenty-eight acres, Caltrans (California transportation agency) told the developers that a new access road to their beach property would be provided when the freeway was built.

In 1975, after the F34S freeway was constructed, the property owners looked but found no access road. The property was worthless, of course, without the access road. When contacted, Caltrans officials were evasive as to why the road had not been constructed. But there *was* a reason. During the trial of the case years later, it was found that the Coastal Commission staff had sent a secret letter to Caltrans asking them not to build the road because the commission wanted to acquire the land for a state park, and it would cost the state more money if the property had an access road. This appeared to be a clear conspiracy of the state to violate the rights of the property owners. Due to the property owners' action a trial resulted, forcing Caltrans to formally condemn the property.

Another issue in this case was a beautiful 250-foot-high sand dune, smaller sand dunes, and a supposedly endangered plant species, the wallflower, in one corner of the property. In the condemnation trial state officials declared that the Coastal Commission would not have permitted development on the property because of the wallflower and other commission policies. Therefore, the property's value was not dependent upon the access road. County and city officials admitted that development would have been permitted if the state had not intervened.

The owners' planner and architect presented plans and models showing how private development could have taken place in a sensitive manner, creating homes for people, tax revenue to the public, and conserving the sand dune and wallflower area at no expense to the public. Also, a beach park of ten acres would have been provided free to the public in the balanced development. The plan (Figures 5–7) illustrates how the state and city government, working in harmony with the developer, could have created an attractive, well-sited public beach park with its facilities built, protected, and maintained at the developer's expense, not the public's.

Instead, the state paid $1.8 million for land that at present there are no funds to improve. Tax revenue will be eliminated forever. The state admitted that it had no plans to protect the sand dunes and wallflowers from the public. Testimony at the trial indicated people were walking over the supposedly sensitive areas and the state was doing nothing to protect the environment of the areas.

The Marina Dunes case illustrates how the state could, with imagination and common sense, keep land productive, provide needed housing, and conserve important beach land for public use, all at little cost to the taxpayers. But in a direct abuse of common sense the commission prevented this, almost as if to say that if they themselves couldn't "save the environment," then no one else could either.

The Lone Star Industries Case

For Lone Star Industries of Moss Landing, a coastal wetlands area approximately 15 miles north of Monterey, the problem was the same as at Marina Dunes, but with a different consideration. The Lone Star Industries' property contained an old smokestack, now used as a navigational aid for ships and airplanes. The company proposed a development on the property that was entirely unrelated to the smokestack. In the hearing of the Coastal Commission, the landowner was asked what it would cost to remove the smokestack, which was considered to be a visual eyesore. The applicant stated that he had no intention of removing the smokestack. It did not form a basis of their application. When pressed, however, the applicant disclosed that the removal of the smokestack would cost $100,000. The Coastal Commission announced that the smokestack could remain and the application proceed, only if the applicant donated $50,000 to a local agency. The extortion was completed when the donation was made.

Ocean View Investors

For Ocean View Investors of Santa Cruz, California, the method of extortion was similar to that used on Lone Star Industries, but this time it was related to the denial of a constitutional right. Ocean View Investors owned a 40-acre parcel. A small part of the western portion of the property touched the beachfront. The planned project included a three-phase development of approximately 350 condominiums starting at the beach and progressing to the farthest point inland. (See Figure 8.) Unfortunately, the owner's plans for development conflicted with the State of California's plans to acquire the entire property.

Any formal public acquisition, pursuant to the United States and California Constitution, requires that the State of California pay "just compensation" for the fair market value of the owners' property. The Coastal Commission decided it could obtain a "park" without compensation, and thus deprive the owners of their constitutional rights.

Ocean View Investors were allowed to proceed with the construction of ninety-seven condominiums on the easternmost inland portion of the property (twelve acres) on the condition that it dedicate, free of cost, the remaining twenty-eight of the forty acres to the State of California and build on the property a forty-car parking lot, a paved access road, a restroom, a stairway, a fence, and landscaping

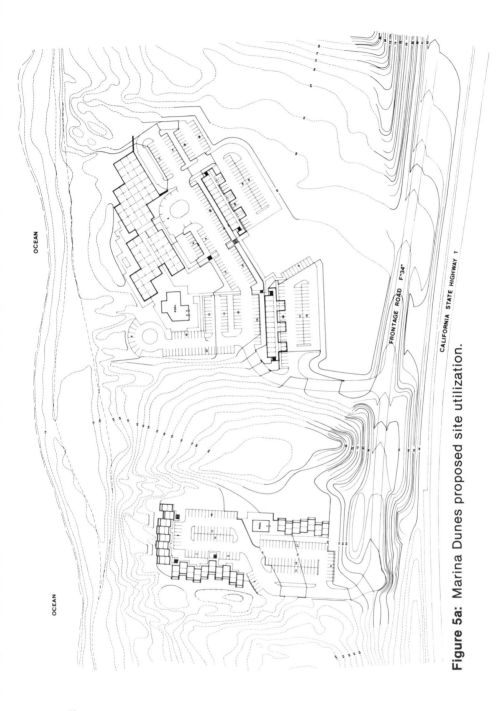

Figure 5a: Marina Dunes proposed site utilization.

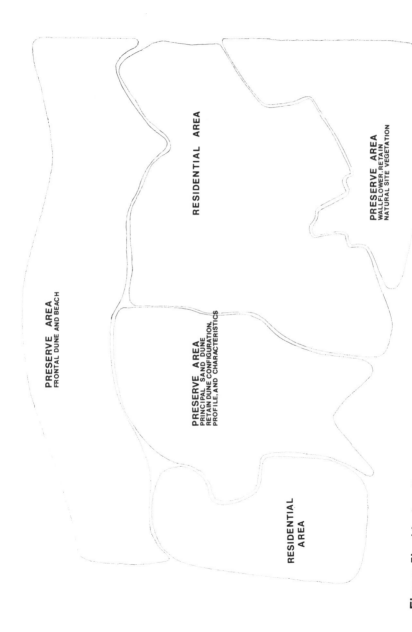

PRESERVE AREA
FRONTAL DUNE AND BEACH

RESIDENTIAL   AREA

PRESERVE AREA
WALLFLOWER-RETAIN
NATURAL SITE VEGETATION

PRESERVE AREA
PRINCIPAL SAND DUNE
RETAIN DUNE CONFIGURATION,
PROFILE, AND CHARACTERISTICS

RESIDENTIAL
AREA

Figure 5b: Marina Dunes possible public and private use of site.

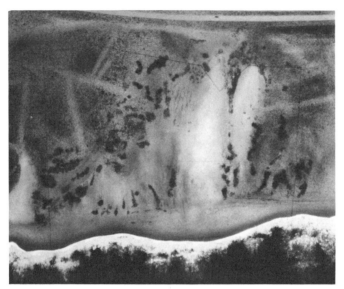

Figure 6: Marina Dunes "before."

Photos courtesy of Scale Model Unlimited.

Figure 7: Marina Dunes "after."

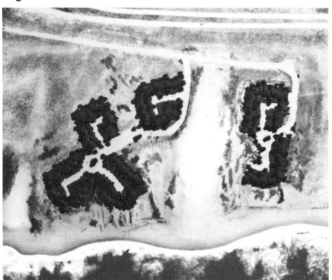

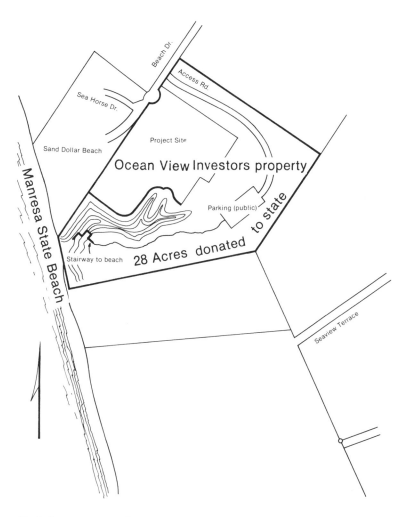

Not drawn to scale

Figure 8:   Ocean View Investors property plan.

and donate $45,000 to the State Department of Parks and Recreation.

It is important to remember that withholding something (permission to build) as a lever for gaining something else (the land dedication) is extortion. If the Coastal Commission was concerned that the development, even partial development, would ruin the ecology they should have taken legal steps to prevent it by denying the permit. Had they wanted the land in order to preserve it, they should have obtained it legally by purchasing it. What they did was obtain it illegally by extortion, which was completed when the dedication was granted.

The Monterey Sand Company

Businesses dependent upon coastal resources have not been exempt from the kind of extortion used on the Ocean View Investors. In the case of Monterey Sand Company, Inc. the extortion was accomplished through "contributions."

In 1978-79, the Monterey Sand Company submitted a request that they be permitted to continue extracting sand from surf and beach areas located in the cities of Marina and Sand City in Monterey County. This application was consistent with the prior use of the property and with Monterey Sand Company's business of producing, sorting, sacking, and selling bulk sand for commercial use. The company relied upon a particular section of the coastline that has naturally sorted sands, cleansed of impurities and polished by surf action. The Coastal Commission admitted that the applicant's development and use of the sand was truly a unique coastal-dependent business. Therefore, the development was found to have a special priority as a coastal-dependent industry under the Coastal Act of 1976.

The Coastal Commission found that the application of Monterey Sand Company was in compliance with the Coastal Act and did not result in any environmental degradation. The commission further found that the business was a unique and highly valuable enterprise to a number of industries along the coast. Nevertheless, the commission concluded that continued sand mining "may" adversely affect the public welfare *some day in the future* as a result of increased shoreline erosion. On that basis, the Coastal Commission required that Monterey Sand Company contribute to the State of California $50,000 for the funding of a study to be done by the state's Coastal Conservancy. In essence, the Monterey Sand Company was forced to fund a government study or face losing their permit to operate.

"Social Engineering"

One of the greatest potential abuses of any government agency is the extent to which its own sense of power can result in enactments and policies that are completely contrary to its own stated goals. In recent years, the Coastal Commission has engaged in "social engineering" by imposing social land use and housing constraints on the basis of "environmental" guidelines. This "social engineering" has taken the form of mandatory low- and moderate-income housing dedications by landowners. In addition, home builders have been forced to dedicate 25 percent and more of all units in their projects to the poor through bizarre restrictive price covenants as a condition of approval. The net effect of this practice has been to artificially drive up the price of all remaining housing units beyond the range of moderate income families.

The Coastal Commission applied a standard that 25 percent of the rooms in a hotel be devoted to people with low income in the development of hotel sites in the state of California. One particular case in Marina del Rey received the wrath of national publications that included the *Christian Science Monitor* and *Wall Street Journal.* In 1979, the Coastal Commission reviewed two applications by one developer for the construction of two hotels in the luxury resort area of Marina del Rey in the county of Los Angeles.

The first hotel, called the Marina Plaza, was to be located on a 3.7-acre site and consist of a 14-story hotel with 400 rooms, apartments, offices, shops, dining and restaurant facilities, and parking. The second development, known as the Marina Belle Hotel, was to be a nine-story, mid-rise hotel with 300 rooms, restaurant, bar, coffee shop, and meeting rooms, also to be located on a 3.7-acre site. However, the conditions imposed by the Coastal Commission rendered both projects economically unfeasible and impractical.

The Coastal Commission required that the Marina Belle Hotel make forty-five rooms available on the weekend for low- or moderate-income persons who earned from "0 to 120 percent of the median income of Los Angeles County." In addition, the hotel was required to provide low- or moderate-cost meals and recreational facilities together with feasible transportation improvements to make the development more available to the intended user population. How the commission gained the right to levy these requirements, which are far afield from any "environmental" considerations, requires mental gymnastics of extraordinary dimension.

The commission required that the other development, Marina Plaza Hotel, be built as a moderate-priced motel of no more than 200 units in which the maximum room rental could not exceed 180 percent of the published rate of a low-priced Motel 6 chain unit and in which the restaurant coffee shop could not charge prices in excess of a neighboring Denny's or Sambo's. In addition, the owner was expected to provide a fifty-bed hostel to be approved by the American Youth Hostel Association of the United States.

The *Christian Science Monitor* suggested that perhaps we all now have a "right to a Rolls Royce." To quote the builder's attorney: "If the poor have a right to luxury hotel rooms, then why not a Rolls Royce or a Caribbean vacation?"

On January 25, 1980, the *Wall Street Journal* stated that "the California Coastal Commission recently raised the art of inclusionary housing to new heights by decreeing that the poor have a statutory right to rent luxury beachfront hotel rooms at half price. . . . The decision flabbergasts the building industry which questioned the logic and fairness of such social engineering."

Nicknamed "the Zip Code Hotel," the Marina Belle, according to its owner, would probably have to determine the poorness of vacationers based on the zip code of their residential address. An editorial of KNXT-TV, Los Angeles, suggested people at the front desk would have to turn in an IRS form to prove their income of the prior year. Or, as the *Commentary* of KABC Television, Los Angeles, suggested on February 4, 1980: "The problem is that once regulations like this start they just don't stop, and where will it go after hotels? So if you're tired of hearing about the aggression of the Soviets in Afghanistan, we thought we'd mention the aggression of the Coastal Commission in Marina del Rey. No violence in the Marina, as there is in Kabul, Afghanistan, but the economic systems to be imposed in both cities have some glaring similarities."

The "Tickled Pink" Case

In Monterey, media response to the Marina del Rey antics of the Coastal Commission was similar. "Will those low-income folks so familiar to federal and state bureaucrats be tickled pink to learn that they soon will be able to get a room at the "Tickled Pink Motor Inn" at the Carmel Highlands for $25 a night."

In response to the application of the developer to add a four-room wing to the Carmel Highlands motel, the Coastal Commission required that one room be set aside for guests at a price in the range of $25 per night, despite the fact that the balance of the rooms would be renting from $39 to $89 a night. A newspaper critic noted: "What's to prevent a fellow who drives up in a Lincoln Continental with a trunkfull of elegant luggage from taking the $25 room?" Apparently nothing. A supervisor from Monterey County questioned, "What if a coastal commissioner drives up in his Cadillac? Can he get the room?"

But even the $25 room at the Highlands Motel was not solidified as a condition until the commission had suggested that as an alternative the landowner donate $5,000 annually to a "coastal access enhancement program to maintain and operate such coastal facilities as parking lots and campgrounds." In response to the owner's representative, who said, "the thing I'm concerned about is I don't know what we're talking about," the chairman of the commission responded, "neither do we." The $25 room was thereafter imposed instead of the $5,000 donation.

Federal Hearings on the Coastal Commission

In January 1980, the Office of Coastal Zone Management, a federal bureaucratic mother organization to the California Coastal Commission, conducted hearings concerning the operation and conduct of the commission. Federal Congressional reviews followed shortly thereafter. In both instances, the public comments on abuse, excesses, and extortion were ignored as the Commission was praised and cited by Robert Knecht, Director of the Federal Office of Coastal Zone Management, as the "flagship of coastal management for the nation."[22]

The coast had been saved, or had it? And at what cost?—not just in dollars but in constitutional rights.

Chapter Four

Save the Environment

The movement to "save the environment" was launched on "Earth Day" in 1970. Voices of preservation soon demanded that forests, coastlines, lakeshores, and marshes be left in a virginal state, devoid of people and activity. Forest and mountain areas were to remain in a wilderness state, visited only by a few backpackers and hikers. Forests were for animals, not lumbermen. The coastland was for the "public," not homes, hotels, or restaurants. Thus emerged a new concept for our lands and waters.

The strong environmental movement that came about in the 1960s and 1970s was obviously needed to prevent deterioration and pollution of our land, air, and water resources. Our nation's underground water supplies, rivers, and lakes needed rehabilitation. Air quality needed attention and regulation on a national scale. Land and natural resources were being abused and needed wiser planning and regulatory systems.

In implementing regulatory controls, however, extreme environmentalists have gone beyond responsible and affordable means and attempted to achieve almost impossible goals, at any price, and without regard to individual constitutional rights.

The federal government's recent high rate of growth in laws, regulations, and expenditures closely parallelled the environmental movement, the controls of local government, and land-use planning. All three are intertwined. In this book, the change of values and goals of the federal government, the growth of the environmental crusade, and their impact on private land-use and civil rights are examined.

America's Changing Environment

There has been a radical change in views toward the environment today, sharply contrasting with those of our Puritan forefathers. Rene Dubos, in his book *The Wooing of Earth,*[23] commented: "When the Puritans arrived in the New World, the huge forests that covered the Atlantic Coast at the time similarly appeared to them as a 'hideous and desolate wilderness full of wilde beastes and wilde men.' " The majority of immigrants who settled in the rest of the American Continent during the following two centuries also regarded the primeval forests with fear and contempt.

During the agricultural development of the United States, our forefathers altered the environment drastically in order to plant orchards and crops, for the earth was a means of survival, a source of food, necessities, and employment. The wilderness was a source of danger, whether from wild animals, hostile Indians or the elements. Settlers cleared land around their homes as a measure of security that enabled them to see approaching hostile humans or animals.

Pursuant to a concept that all men had a natural right to acquire land, federally owned land was made available to people for settlement and cultivation, through the Homestead Act of 1862. Government expressed little concern in this early period of America's growth to the environmental characteristics of land or to its suitability for private use.

As America industrialized and people moved from farms and villages into the cities for factory and office jobs, the character and problems of America changed. Poorly designed and overcrowded buildings generated health, sanitation, and fire problems, which in turn necessitated initial government regulations. Soon cities and counties adopted regulations for land and building use within their communities without the involvement of state or federal governments.

James Sterling Young, in his book, *The Washington Community: 1820-1828,*[24] states: "The early government was an organization of warriors and revenue collectors. Approximately 95 percent of its manpower was assigned to military functions and to the production of revenue. . . ." Thus, the national government was concerned primarily with national defense, minting money, collecting revenue, postal service, foreign relations, lighthouses for navigation, and law enforcement. The environment was not a consideration of the federal government, and the issue of land-use planning was a concern of local government alone.

The Nature of Environmental Problems

In altering the environment, the settlers of our country created new land-use patterns that were both functional and attractive. The New England villages such as Lexington and Concord, along with early communities in the South, generally were aesthetic and harmonious with nature. However, settlers drastically altered the existing environment with plants, as well as buildings. New species of trees and other plants were brought to America from other parts of the world and planted in orderly groves of citrus, apple, walnut, and other varieties, thus altering the landscape. Farm building complexes and communities were carefully placed in settings that are attractive even to this day.

Despite isolated instances of wasteful slaughter of animals for hides, furs, and feed, most early Americans worked in harmony with animals and plants, which were their source for transportation, food, and clothing. Trees and plants provided materials for shelter, heat, fences, and food to sustain their survival. Plants, in turn, were cultivated and aided by man. Animals were also nurtured by the new settlers, and they improved in quality and numbers.

Unfortunately, with urbanization came new industrial complexes and crowded, ugly clusters of accompanying labor housing. Overcrowding and blight became a resulting eyesore of much industrialization. Irresponsible and careless industrial operations contributed to the pollution of rivers, lakes, and underground water supplies. Industrial and human wastes soon poured into once-clear lakes, rivers, and oceans, harming wildlife, plant, and water resources. Conflicts between communities over water for drinking, fishing, and waste disposal soon developed. The accumulation of people in concentrated areas and the increasing effects of automobile and industrial use generated air pollution problems that could not be controlled within municipal boundaries.

The beauty and attraction of our shoreline, oceans, lakes, and rivers brought concentrations of housing and commercial and industrial facilities, all generating a myriad of problems. Miami Beach, once a beautiful section of coastline, soon became overcrowded with buildings, and the natural attractiveness of the area was degraded by a wall of highrise structures that cast cold, dark shadows on the once sunny beach that tourists came to enjoy.

Power plants and industrial complexes competed for land with residential and recreational uses on the Pacific, Gulf, and Atlantic coastlines. Due to arrogance and an ignorance of the effect of toxic wastes on the environment, explosives, chemicals, mustard gas, and other pollutants were dumped indiscriminantly for many years in marshes, lakes, and the ocean. As the population grew and communities expanded, man's delicate interrelationship with the earth and our environment became more and more apparent.

During the 1930s, the New Deal introduced federal legislation concerned with employment, health, and housing. A "save the city" movement flourished in the 1950s as issues of civil rights and poverty dominated the nation. The rapid industrialization and expansion of the urban population in the 50s and 60s generated new problems that resulted in the "Environmental Decade" of the 1970s. So began our environmental movement. A result has been excessive government legislation designed to protect the environment and resources of our country.

The Federal Environmental Machine

The National Environmental Policy Act of 1969 was followed by a mass of federal legislation aimed at solving the nation's environmental problems. This act was followed by the Clean Air Act, the Clean Water Act, Federal Highways Act, Coastal Zone Management Act, Toxic Substance Control Act, Occupational Safety and Health Act, Surface Mining Control and Reclamation Act, Endangered Species Act, Resource Conservation and Recovery Act, Noise Control Act, Safe Drinking Water Act, Federal Land Policy and Management Act, National Forest Management Act, and many others. (See Appendix A for descriptions of major acts.)

Federal environmental legislation government has fallen generally into the following groups: (1) protection of natural resources, (2) pollution control, (3) urban planning and housing, (4) management of federal lands, (5) agricultural programs, (6) energy regulation, and (7) general environmental planning and coordination.

This legislation had a tremendous impact on local government planning, costs and administration, as well as on private land use.

Impact on Local Planning

During the 1950s and 1960s, federal programs tended to bypass state agencies and work more directly with regional or local jurisdictions. During the 1970s the trend changed and federal programs began operating through the state governments, establishing a totally new

73

bureaucracy. Because of this, local jurisdictions rapidly lost control and authority over land-use and environmental planning to federal and state agencies that are frequently insensitive to local problems and needs.

An example of this federal and state interference in local government can be seen in Ventura County, California (discussed in chapter 5). In an analysis of federal and state programs involved in land-use planning, cities and counties found that their traditional planning authority was impacted directly or indirectly by over twenty federal and state agencies or authorities. City urban renewal officials and other local government agencies found their powers also usurped.

The most significant trend in environmental legislation has been more and more federal involvement and less and less local and county control. The effect of this can be seen in several developments.

1. Federal land-use goals emphasize the acquisition and management of land, while state legislation usually reflects a regulatory orientation.

2. There appears to be a trend toward the distribution of federal grants at the state level rather than at a local or community level.

3. Most of the regional or area-wide planning agencies established and influenced by federal inducement-type legislation have in general remained as they were initially—advisory in nature.

An Investigation of Federal Policy

Congress' enthusiasm to solve the environmental problems with legislation has generated so many problems for local government, public utilities, commercial enterprises, private landowners, and taxpayers that investigations by the federal government were initiated in the late 1970s to alleviate the situation.

The massive environmental legislation accelerated an old problem of "uncoordinated federal policies." As a result, President Carter in his environmental message to Congress in 1977 established the President's Interagency Task Force on Environmental Data and Monitoring Programs. The Task Force was to "recommend improvements that would make these programs more effective."[25]

The Task Force's group involved with Land and Natural Resources found that "no cohesive federal land and natural resource policy exists today. Federal policy is highly fragmented."[26] The task force identified approximately twenty-five agencies and over seventy legislative acts that influenced land and natural resources in environmental policies. They also found that federal policies were in conflict in four major areas:

1. Management of federal lands
2. Pollution control
3. Resource development
4. Resource protection and preservation

The U.S. government owns over 750 million acres of land, or about one-third of the nation's total land area. This large land ownership gives the federal government an opportunity in many parts of the country to dominate local land-use policies and regulations. In the past, the policies of the federal government tended to encourage westward expansion, generate income, and produce funds through the disposal of government land holdings. However, since the creation of the national parks and forests system at the turn of the 20th century, the federal land-use policy became increasingly complex.

The Land and Natural Resources working group discovered that land and natural resource policies in the United States had been established historically on an *ad hoc* approach that generated an all-encompassing dominance of land, surface, subsurface, and air. Unfortunately, Congress failed to balance multiple uses of federal lands, thus creating conflicts for priority between mining, timber, recreation, and the wilderness. This conflict was only one of many that afflicted the inter-relationship of so many overlapping environmental acts.

The report further stated that the complexity of land-use policies necessitated "the recent enactment of major comprehensive land-use planning legislation designed to provide definite norms for public lands management."[27]

There is a wide variety of planning mechanisms incorporated piecemeal into federal legislation. These were devised to prevent conflicts (but have usually contributed to it). The federal government's mechanisms to implement land-use policies include:

- Financial assistance
- Agency coordination
- "Comprehensive" planning
- Fact-finding and information sharing
- Delegation to state and local authorities

- Tax incentives
- Technical assistance
- Regulation
- Acquisition
- Enforcement

The Task Force found the federal government's role in land-use planning divided into three distinct areas: (1) land-use planning on federally owned lands; (2) activities of the various federal agencies that impact land use; and (3) federal programs that attempt to influence state and local planning.

In the United States, land and resource management traditionally has been a state and local function. In the 1970s, with federal environmental legislation being passed, Congress became more interested in gaining control over state and local land-use jurisdictions. Normally, the federal government implemented its policies in the area of land management by financial inducements that would encourage desired state, regional, and local actions rather than by direct federal involvement. Inducements consisted of grant and loan programs that required local jurisdictions to perform planning functions as a condition of financial aid.

The enactment of the Federal Water Pollution Control Act (Clean Water Act) in 1972 created a semblance of opposition from local governments that interpreted the provisions as disguised federal land-use planning.

Various federal acts of the 1970s encouraged citizen involvement in environmental protection, including legal actions by citizens to enforce environmental standards against violators. (Often, the "violator" was the government agency charged with enforcing the statute.) Projects of the Corps of Engineers, state highway department, the TVA and others were challenged and delayed. Many organizations such as the Sierra Club, National Wildlife Federation, and Friends of the Earth led other citizen groups in the implementation of the laws. The National Resources Defense Council and the Environmental Defense Fund were also formed for the purpose of monitoring the implementation of the laws by federal agencies.

The Task Force report stated that there was a "quiet revolution in land-use control" and that land now tends to be used as a resource, not just as a commodity. Federal and state legislatures seem to favor the legislative approach to land-use controls in the U.S. and accept the "quiet revolution in land-use control."

Federal Government Growth and Local Impact

Federal environmental legislation was often criticized for being both ineffectual and interfering with local government. These facts are clearly stated in a publication of the Federal Advisory Commission on Intergovernmental Relations in 1980 entitled "A Crisis of Confidence and Competence."[28] This report blames Congress for many unmanageable, wasteful, and unaccountable systems of aid programs. It indicates that the present dysfunctional (disordered) situation of government has brought about a "state of total confusion."

The commission stated that federal officials play different roles: "Presidents act almost as frequently in a mayoral [local] or gubernatorial [state] role as a national presidential one, and Congress plays [the role of] municipal and county council almost as often as it plays the role of national deliberative body. It has produced a situation where no level or set of officials is performing the functions it is best suited to perform."

The commission found that Congress had refused to assume full responsibility for functions that should be purely national. Congress is also equally unwilling to relinquish matters that should be strictly local. The commission stated that:

> A rather fanciful form of Federalism, then, has emerged. Basic policies in most program areas appear to be made in Washington, and their implementation is achieved through decisions, orders, mandates, conditions, regulations, and the lure of federal loot for twelve million state and local civil servants. And in the end, the fancy becomes caprice—caprice because the subnational governments, their elected officials and bureaucracies are capable of highly differentiated responses to all this in terms of compliance, cooperation, participation, and conflict. Equally fanciful is any notion that the federal aid system as a whole protects the interests of the needy or equalizes levels of public services. Questions of equity are largely ignored in the scramble for benefits.

The advisory commission noted that the characteristics of the federal government are:

1. Its great growth since the 1930s;
2. Its assumption of new roles for providing social benefits, managing the economy, protecting the environment, and pursuing other innovative goals—so that now it is involved in virtually every func-

tion of government;

3. The dramatic growth of the federal aid system in the past two decades;
4. The mounting burden of federal regulations, paperwork, and intrusion into the activities of virtually every individual, business, nonprofit corporation, and state and local government.

Figures 9 and 10 show the growth and cost of federal regulation by type. Note the energy and environmental costs. The growth in federal aid can be seen in Figures 11 and 12. The growth of federal regulations is illustrated in Figures 13, 14, 15, and 16. The number of federal mandates and pages contained in the Federal Register and Code of Federal Regulations[29] are shown in Figures 17 and 18, respectively.

Basically the same findings were discovered in the 1977–78 report of the Advisory Commission on Intergovernmental Relations (ACIR), a study of intergovernmental grant system, which states: "Never has the maze of fiscal, functional, regulatory, and administrative links between and among the federal government, the states, and all substate units been more complex, costly, and convoluted than it is now."[30]

Much of the federal government's local influence comes through the General Revenue Sharing Program. ACIR estimated that 37,704 state and local governments out of 38,776 such governments receive revenue sharing payments.[31]

Of the estimated 26,000 special districts in the U.S., about 10,000 (38 percent) are eligible for federal aid. Approximately 63,000 of the country's 80,000 units of state and local government (80 percent) probably are receiving federal funds. There are probably another 2,000 substate regional organizations.

The ACIR quotes from a study done by James E. Krier and Edmond Ursin on pollution and policy in California[32] that "pollution policy is national policy and the states are little more than reluctant minons mandated to do the dirty work—to implement federal directives often distasteful at the local level."

In a study entitled "The Costs of Government Regulation of Business," Murray L. Weidenbaum summed up the views of individuals, business, and state and local governments toward federal influence in Figure 19, "Symptoms of the Burdens of Federal Influence."

The lack of success of federal intervention in environmental mat-

Figure 9: Creation of federal regulatory agencies (by type) graphed cumulatively over time.

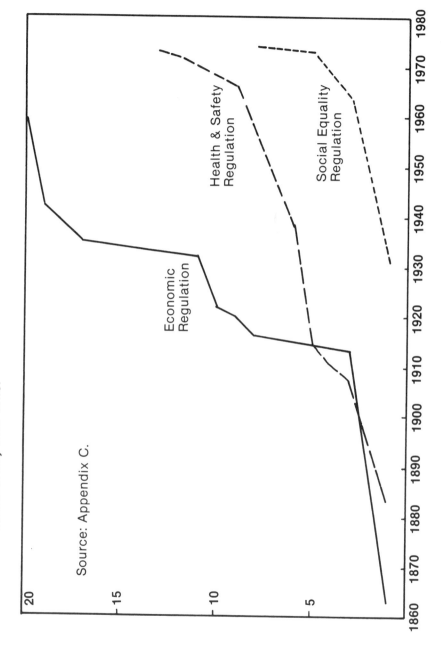

Source: Appendix C.

Figure 10: Administrative costs of 41 federal regulatory agencies, by type (fiscal years; dollars in billions).

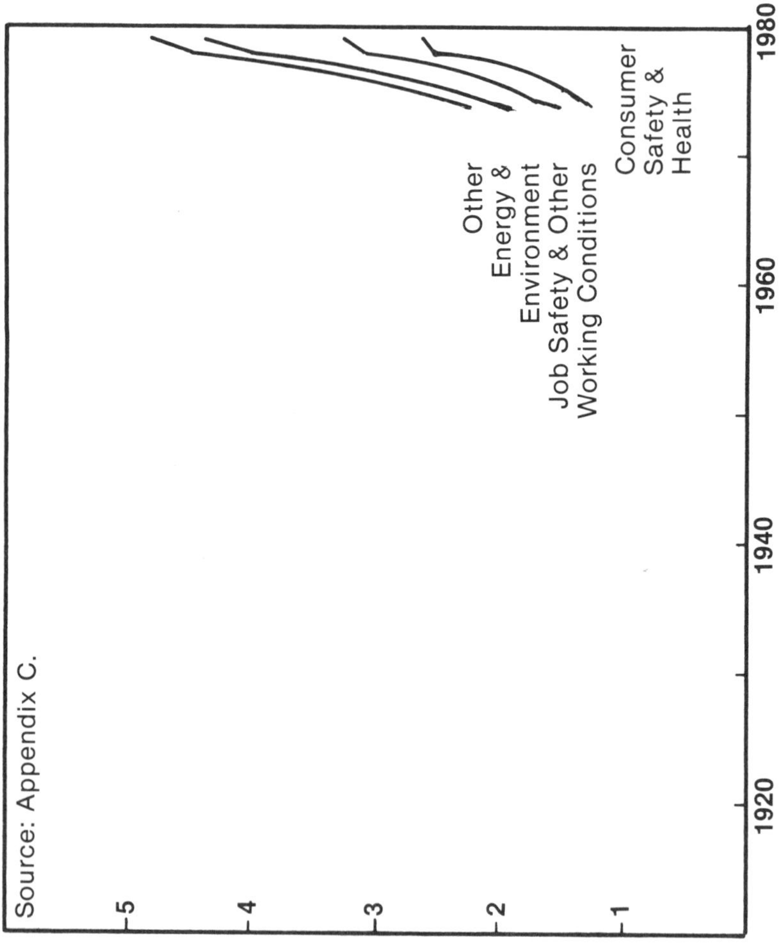

Source: Appendix C.

Other
Energy &
Environment
Job Safety & Other
Working Conditions

Consumer
Safety &
Health

1920   1940   1960   1980

5
4
3
2
1

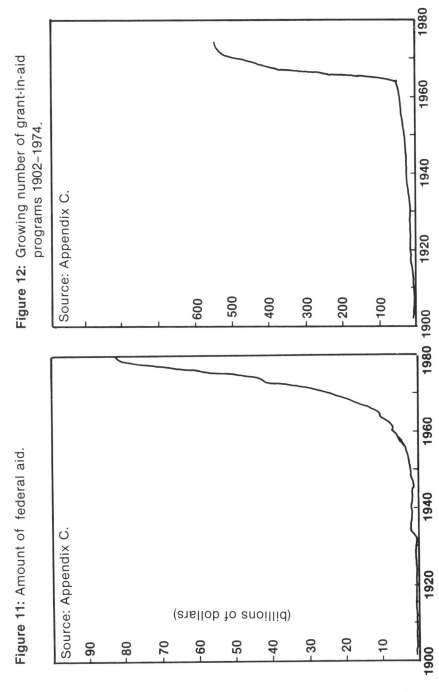

Figure 12: Growing number of grant-in-aid programs 1902–1974.

Source: Appendix C.

Figure 11: Amount of federal aid.

Source: Appendix C.

(billions of dollars)

Figure 13: Creation of federal regulatory agencies (graphed cumulatively).

Source: Appendix C.
45
40
35
30
25
20
15
10
5
1900
1940
1980

Figure 14: Funds budgeted for major federal regulatory agencies.

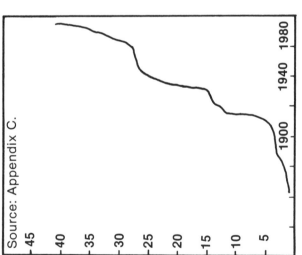

Source: Center for the Study of American Business, Washington University, St. Louis, MO, as reported in *Nation's Business,* July 1979, p. 8.
6
5
4
3
2
1
1900
1920
1940
1960
1980

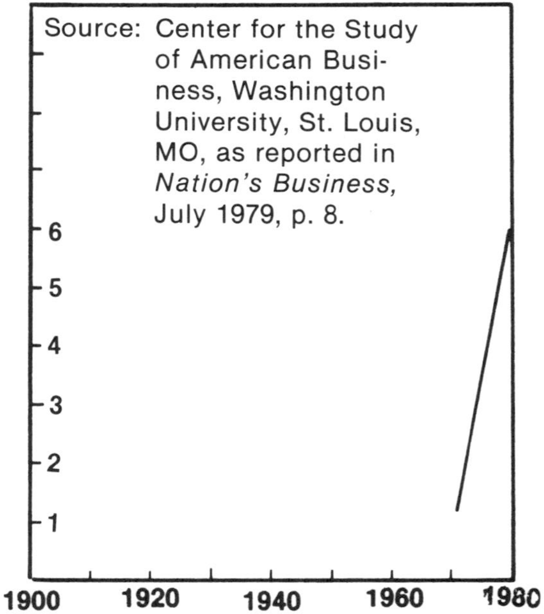

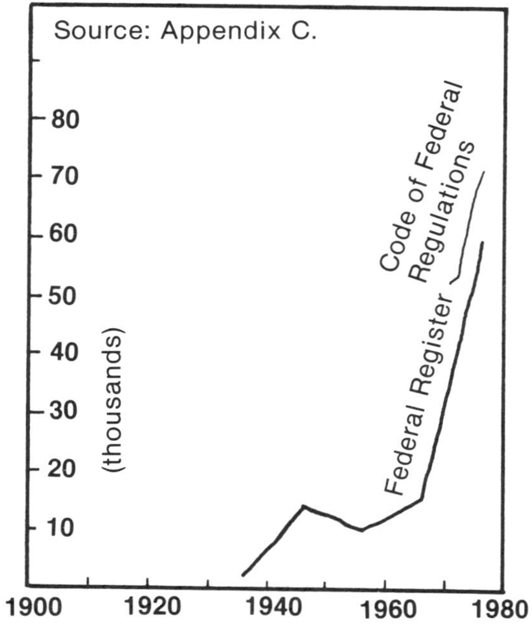

Figure 16: Federal mandates imposed on local governments.

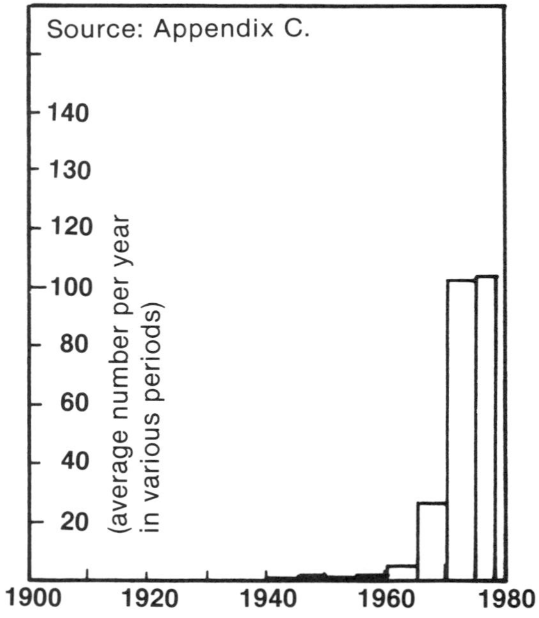

Source: Appendix C.

Figure 15: Number of pages published annually in the Federal Register and the number of pages in the Code of Federal Regulations.

Source: Appendix C.

Figure 17: Number of federal mandates by estimated year of imposition, by direct orders and conditions of aid, 1941–1978.

Year	Federal Register	Code of Federal Regulations
1936	2,355	—
1946	14,736	—
1956	10,528	—
1966	16,850	—
1970	20,036	54,105
1971	25,447	54,487
1972	28,928	61,035
1973	35,592	64,852
1974	42,422	69,270
1975	60,221	72,200

Source: Lovell, Katherine, et. al. *Federal and State Mandating to Local Government: Impact and Issues.* Riverside, CA, University of California, 1979 draft, p. 71.

Figure 18: Pages contained in the federal register and code of federal regulations, selected years, 1936–1975.

Years	Direct Orders	Conditions of Aid	Total
1941–45	—	—	—
1946–50	8	—	8
1951–55	—	2	2
1956–60	2	2	4
1961–65	5	24	29
1966–70	43	92	135
1971–75	109	559	668
1976–78	57	354	911

Source: Fiorina, Morris P. *Congress: Keystone of the Washington Establishment.* New Haven, CT, Yale University Press, 1977, p. 93; and the Public interest, Number 47, National Affairs, Inc., New York, NY, Spring 1977, p. 50.

ters was stated by Charles L. Schultze, then chairman of the President's Council of Economic Advisors. He wrote: "Efforts to improve the environment, while far from a failure, are unnecessarily expensive and increasingly bogged down in Rube Goldberg regulations, legal snarks, and games between regulators and industry as enforcement deadlines draw near."[33]

The commission found that federal government had entered the urban planning arena agressively and created more problems than they solved. Urbanist Louis H. Masotti states:

> An urban policy in America, by and large, has been designed to be therapeutic, i.e., to treat symptoms of the urban malaise rather than to uncover its fundamental causes and to engage in preventive action. It is clear that since the discovery of the urban crisis in the early 1960s, our approach has been to develop more programs, create more bureaucracy, and spend more money in an effort to stem the tide of urban decay; and most of the behavior was a political response to pressure from the cities and their advocates. For the most part, the results of all this activity has been to develop a programmatic, bureaucratic, institutionalized failure. In general, the cities and their residents are less well off than they were before the flurry of urban policies. Those policies have been ineffective and inefficient in pursuit of the ostensible goals—the improvement of the quality of urban lives and the support of cities as economic entities.[34]

The ACIR, made up of twenty-six members, consists of members of Congress, officials from the executive branch of the federal government, governors and legislators, local mayors, elected county officials, and private citizens. The commission felt that "neither public officials nor the general public comprehend fully the new complexities of domestic public policy or adequate control, or even check the myriad forces that have generated it." The commission further indicated that the myriad programs have become so intertwined among the state, local, and federal governments that no government can adequately deal with them.

In general, the commission felt that the federal governmental system was out of control and that this left the electorate "frustrated, fearful, alienated and/or angry. The system has become highly incomprehensible, even to those whose job it is to have an overall understanding of it."

SYMPTOMS OF THE BURDENS OF FEDERAL INFLUENCE
(as frequently expressed by affected parties)

Individuals

Federal taxes are too high!

Federal tax forms are too complicated!

It takes too long and is too hard to fill them out!

Some federal programs are demeaning!

Federal benefits are inadequate!

Federal protections from bad business practices are inadequate!

Certain types of basic needs are not being addressed at all by federal programs!

The federal government is too remote!

Congress is too insensitive!

Federal program administrators are insensitive and ignorant of the system they work under!

The federal courts are simplistic, overly assertive, and overbearing!

The federal government is unable to set realistic priorities; it can only orchestrate interest group pressures!

Businesses

The federal government is costing us money; reducing profits!

Federal paperwork is too burdensome and much of it is unnecessary!

Too much time is spent keeping records, filing reports, and responding to government surveys!

The federal government is increasing the costs of our products!

Federal regulation is reducing competition!

The federal government is causing inflation!

The federal government is reducing productivity!

The federal government is slowing invention, innovation, and entrepreneurial activity!

Figure 19: Symptoms of the burdens of federal influence (as frequently expressed by affected parties).

The federal government is slowing capital formation!

The federal government is slowing business volume and employment!

Federal burdens discriminate against small businesses, making it hard for them to form and continue to exist!

State and Local Governments

The federal government is altering our own priorities!

The federal government allows too little state and local discretion concerning how to meet national objectives!

We must spend too much time (and money) on federal red tape and paperwork!

Federal assistance is hard to get and administer! It requires too much grantsmanship!

The federal government mandates too many activities on us without paying for them! (or with inadequate reimbursement!)

The federal government makes too many decisions affecting state and local governments, without consulting them!

The federal government shows little capacity in implementing its own programs, but pretends to possess it with ours!

Sources: Murray L. Weidenbaum, *The Costs of Government Regulation of Business,* A study prepared for the Subcommittee on Economic Stabilization of the Joint Economic Committee, 95th Cong., 2nd Sess., Washington, DC, U.S. Government Printing Office, April 10, 1978; Advisory Commission on Intergovernmental Relations, *The Intergovernmental Grant System as Seen by Local, State, and Federal Officials,* A-54, Washington, DC, U.S. Government Printing Office, March 1977; Advisory Commission on Intergovernmental Relations. *Changing Public Attitudes on Governments and Taxes: 1979,* S-8, Washington, DC, U.S. Government Printing Office, 1979.

The Federal Environmentalists in Action

A new breed of environmentally oriented government officials infiltrated agencies concerned with environmental matters. Dedicated to saving the environment, these extremists often ride roughshod over the individual rights and interests of citizens. They frequently request conditions that are unauthorized by law, establish procedures that cause project hearing delays and added costs, cancel meetings, and generally slow down projects being processed for approval—all to change projects radically or stop them. If individual and property rights are to be abandoned, shouldn't we at least vote on it?

In his article entitled "The Coercive Utopians: Their Hidden Agenda,"[35] Dr. H. Peter Metzger alluded to a new Washington "spoils system" made up of environmental elitists and self-righteous zealots. "Like most zealots," Metzger wrote, "these environmentalists are very different from ordinary people. True believers all, they exude party line and exclude from serious attention any person or opinion that doesn't conform with theirs."

He quotes Lewellyn King, publisher of *The Energy Daily:* "There is a feeling that bigotry clothed in righteousness has taken over and is fouling the processes of government." He continues, "It came about because President Carter has introduced into public service a new kind of individual not formerly part of the Washington scene. They are the environmentalists, the consumer-advocates and others from what is loosely called the counterculture." One Washington wag referred to them as the "environ-necks."

Dr. Metzger found that President Carter appointed to subcabinet posts many former "public interest" lawyers, consumerists, civil rights workers, and especially environmental advocates. He found that, although there were not many, less than one hundred in all, they held very powerful jobs: fourteen key White House assistants (including the President's chief speech writer) came out of the "public interest" movement. Dr. Metzger continued, "Former anti-energy activists are now [were] four assistant attorney generals in the Department of Justice and assistant secretaries in the Departments of Health, Education, and Welfare and Commerce, Interior, Agriculture, and Housing and Urban Development." He states that public interest advocates for those who share the concerns had been appointed to chair the Equal Employment Opportunity Commission, the National Highway Traffic Safety Administration, the Occupational Safety and Health Administration, ACTION and the Federal Trade Commission.

Metzger indicated that ranking jobs in the Environmental Protection Agency in the Department of the Interior had gone to men and women who have sued in courts and lobbied the government for conservation, protection of wildlife, and clear air and water. All three members of the Council on Environmental Quality came from environmental advocacy organizations.

Mr. Ric Davidge, former assistant to Senator Stevens of Alaska, stated that during the late 70s a large number of important congressmen and senators had young environmental elitists, with little work experience or first-hand information on the problems of the country, advising them on national legislation and policy.

Metzger compares environmental advocates, to other utopian movement leaders who "have much preferred tearing down the existing order rather than being bothered by the grimy details of how to replace what they've destroyed." They want to "strangle our society by stopping everything necessary to our nation's growth, i.e.: water, coal and nuclear power, land use, and new industry." The coercive utopians are proceeding toward their goals by the "hidden agenda." They used court and government administrative delays as a means to curb energy development (in the name of review and evaluation).

Typical of the environmentalists' tactics was the implementation of Carter's eighteen-dam "hit list" that recommended not funding water development dams in the western states. When the western states and agencies complained of the "hit list," a water policy review was announced. It was followed by a suit that barred the Department of the Interior from sending any water policy recommendations to Carter until completion of a long series of hearings and impact statements. This added at least another two years before any new water development policy could even be announced.

The Fryingpan-Arkansas Water Diversion Project, which was to supply supplemental water for about 500,000 people in southeastern Colorado, had been planned for about twenty-five years. The project, almost completed after an expenditure of $325 million was jolted in June of 1979. In a surprise move, a "legal opinion" by Leo M. Krulitz, solicitor of the United States Department of the Interior, brought the Fryingpan-Arkansas Project to a halt. According to Dr. Metzger, based on the request of a single private person from Aspen and without any consultation with Colorado state officials, Krulitz alone decided to shut down the project until new congressional legislation was created. Felix Aparks, Director of Colorado's Water

Conservation Board, responded, "Incredible, unbelievable!" The Fryingpan legal advisor, attorney Charles Beise, responded that the action was "a complete distortion, wholly unsupportable, completely lacking in background."

Another project delayed by an antigrowth Carter appointee was the Foothills Water Treatment Plant for Denver. The appointed Regional Environmental Protection Agency (EPA) Director, Alan Merson, found an "endangered red herring," the "Montana skipper," a butterfly that was claimed to be endangered by the construction of the new water treatment plant. The delays caused the cost of the Foothills Water Project to grow from $73 million to $135 million. To avoid describing the situation as a "conspiracy," government antitrust lawyers used the phrase "conscious parallelism."

Snail Darter v. Tellico Dam

Indicative of this attitude was the five-year battle over the snail darter fish and Tellico Dam. Construction on the almost completed dam was held up for five years when the snail darter fish was declared an endangered species. Only after Congress and President Carter exempted the Tellico Dam Project from the Endangered Species Act in September 1979 was the $130 million dam completed.

Colorado Squawfish

A similar situation can be seen in Utah, with the Colorado squawfish. The Colorado squawfish, considered an ugly and tasteless fish, will possibly hold up construction of a dam on Utah's White River. Mr. Robert Shields, area manager for the Fish and Wildlife Service, stated that "it appears that construction of the dam could jeopardize the survival of the squawfish."

However, Utah officials call the small squawfish "a trash fish," and for years have held it in low esteem. It is ironic that earlier, officials killed a number of squawfish in the White River to make room for gamefish such as trout and bass. Unfortunately, their actions helped put the squawfish on the federal government's endangered species list and may jeopardize the dam project.

Utah officials are angry and flabbergasted at the situation. Jim Buckler, a natural resources coordinator for the State of Utah, stated that "on the one hand, Congress gives us the Energy Security Act, which says to develop synthetic fuels; on the other hand they hand us the Endangered Species Act which stops us cold. The whole thing's crazy.''

This feeling is echoed by many who are caught in the maze of regulations and restrictions that are often contradictory and result from radically restrictive attitudes towards our resources at a time when there is more and more demand for their use.

It appeared that this conscious parallelism was in operation between the environmentalists and the government. While the EPA was working to stop the Foothills Water Project in Denver, six large private environmental pressure groups filed suit at the same time against the EPA in Washington, D.C., to stop the project.

RARE II

Another area in which elite environmentalists operated successfully was the Department of Interior's "RARE II" program. ("RARE II" stands for "Roadless Area Review and Evaluation, Second Time," agricultural roads are discounted.) Through this program, the Department of Interior through 1980 withdrew sixty-eight million acres of federal land from development of any kind, pending a decision on whether or not it should be given a "wilderness" status. A "wilderness" area classification bans commercial exploration and the use of any motor vehicles. However, a review of the wilderness areas has been underway for almost fifteen years.

The use of RARE II appears to be a movement of the preservationists who want federal land to be preserved and not utilized for minerals or energy source development. Carter's Department of Energy considered 40 percent of the land locked up by RARE II of "major interest" for energy development. It is estimated that the Overthrust Belt (a geological area) in the Rocky Mountain region contains four billion barrels of oil and fourteen trillion cubic feet of natural gas. No drilling could take place on federal land within the Overthrust Belt area under the Carter Interior Department until it decided what land would be declared a "wilderness" area.

The RARE II policy also stopped lumbering activities in these areas. The mills that depend on the natural forest timber, such as Kaibab in Eagle, Colorado, were threatened with shutdowns. In the Kaibab area alone, the Forest Service estimates a potential 78 million board feet timber harvest, but limited the 1979 sales to 10.8 million board feet. It is interesting that the government's director for the RARE II inventory was a Carter appointee, George Davis of the U.S.

Forest Service. Dr. Metzger states that before Davis entered the government, he was executive director of the Wilderness Society. He also points out that the final RARE II responsibility action belonged to M. Rupert Culter, Assistant Secretary of Agriculture. Before Carter appointed him to that job, he was a high official in the Wilderness Society. This could be another example of "conscious parallelism."

SOHIO Debacle

In a proposed project in which Southern Standard Oil of Ohio (SOHIO) proposed to buy old pipeline that was used to carry natural gas from Texas to California and convert it to pump oil in the opposite direction, SOHIO was to construct a new marine terminal in Long Beach and off-load Alaskan oil from tankers into the pipeline. The oil terminal was estimated to cost SOHIO one-half billion dollars. Due to an EPA requirement called an "offset requirement," the EPA conditioned SOHIO to pay $78 million for the construction and fifteen-year maintenance of a new scrubber for a Southern California Edison smokestack, the emissions of which are currently in full compliance with the law. Also, SOHIO was required to pay another $5 million to thirteen local dry cleaners to help them clean up their hydrocarbon emissions furthur, and they too were presently in compliance with California's air pollution laws.

It came to light that SOHIO, after complying with the EPA's tough conditions, needed more than 700 federal, state, and local permits and a favorable outcome from a public referendum in Long Beach to permit the city of Long Beach to lease space to SOHIO for its terminal. It seems incredible that a country needing oil so badly can make private enterprise go through such impossible hurdles. After spending millions of dollars, SOHIO came to the conclusion that the project should be abandoned.

Influence on Foreign Policies

An article in *Harper's* refers to the environmental imperialism as "exporting pettifoggery." Some extreme environmentalists, not satisfied with controlling the domestic environment, also want to control federal activities and investment in foreign countries. Recently there was a series of lawsuits by environmental organizations attempting to force all federal agencies involved with foreign developments to meet the National Environmental Policy Act (NEPA) impact statement requirements.

The Natural Resources Defense Council (NRDC), generally thought of as an antigrowth, antibusiness organization, sought a court order to make the American Export-Import Bank comply with the requirements of NEPA. In Washington D.C., a federal judge twice prohibited the Federal Highway Administration from continuing further work on the 250-mile Darien Gap Highway through Panama and Colombia on grounds that its environmental impact statement was greatly deficient.

In another case, a loan was stopped to Indonesia that would have allowed the purchase of twenty-four dredges for the purpose of assisting the cultivation of rice and other staple crops for human consumption. The suit was successful, pointing to dangers of siltation, destruction to fisheries, and the loss of some wildlife habitat. Again, there was more reverence for fish and wildlife than for human life in a part of the world desperate for food.

Council On Environmental Quality

Also demanding a broad environmental control over the world was President Carter's Council on Environmental Quality (CEQ). The council proposed requirements that would force all federal agencies to assess the environmental impact on all foreign countries of major federal actions abroad. Their proposed rules applied to nuclear export licenses, aid projects, and many American export-import bank loans.

The impact of this proposed policy would mean that once a foreign state decided it wanted a project in its country it would have to comply with the U.S. NEPA as a condition for trading with the United States. When faced with preparing environmental impact statements for all projects, foreign countries would very likely trade elsewhere and forget the United States.

These proposals are very authoritarian. One wonders who would propose such rules. President Carter's chairman of CEQ, Gus Speth, one of the three board members, was a founder of the antigrowth, antibusiness NRDC, a public-interest law firm, and worked for it before joining CEQ. Other CEQ members who were or are dedicated environmentalists include: Russell Train, an EPA administrator and later a president of the World Wildlife Fund; Russell Peterson, head of the National Audubon Society; Jane Yarn who served on many national and state environmental advisory boards; and Robert H. Harris, a scientist formerly with the Environmental Defense Fund.

It's interesting that the NRDC and the Sierra Club Legal Defense Fund sued the American Export-Import Bank for failure to comply with the NEPA. The suit was filed apparently because the export-import bank was granting loans to foreign countries for American nuclear power plants without first filing an environmental impact statement for the foreign country.

The Justice Department assigned Assistant Attorney General James M. Moorman to represent the export-import bank in the suit. Mr. Moorman was the executive director of and attorney for the Sierra Club's Legal Defense Fund before joining the Justice Department as a Carter appointee. His office then defended the Department of Interior in the *NRDC* v. *Hughes* case, in which the Department of the Interior lost to NRDC.

It was while he was executive director of the Sierra Club's Legal Defense Fund that the Sierra Club filed its own suit against the Atomic Energy Commission (AEC) and the American Export-Import Bank to stop nuclear reactor exports. NRDC and the Sierra Club jointly sued the government ten times while Moorman was the Sierra Club's executive director, before he became a Carter appointee. His office later "defended" the federal government against the NRDC, a case the Sierra Club helped to create.

With the addition of lawyers and advocates from two of the largest environmental public interest law foundations, NRDC and the Environmental Defense Fund, it is not surprising EPA documents carry their philosophies. In one document, advice was given to citizen groups to carry their environmental struggles to the courts. The documents indicated that they should get the names of competent, experienced attorneys, from organizations that specialize in environmental law, such as the National Resources Defense Fund, Inc. or the Environmental Defense Fund.

Environmental groups, although against nuclear power plants, mineral exploration, and most mining and dam projects, are frequently also against the construction of conventional power plants and other means to obtain energy for the nation. One wonders if environmental extremists are really concerned with improving the environment or preventing energy development.

In March of 1979 the Environmental Defense Fund (EDF) sued to stop construction of all seventy-seven conventional power plants started in the United States since 1977. That was the year the new Clean Air Act Amendments became law. As a result of the act's requirement that the "best available pollution control technology" be installed in each plant, the EDF claims that hearings were not held to determine that this was the case.

The delay of the construction of the seventy-seven plants probably will not mean less pollution when they are on stream. It will mean, however, that the cost of energy will be higher in the areas where the plants will be built.

A further example of the new arrogant and self-righteous attitude of recent environment appointees in the federal government is shown by Gus Speth, while Chairman of the Council on Environmental Quality at the Environmental Decade Conference in 1980. He addressed the conference with a speech entitled "A Nation of Conservers." "If we look at the recalcitrants and the adversaries of environmental quality, we see a regrouping of forces, a reassertion of economic clout in cold-blooded exploitation of such fundamental national character traits as suspicion of government interference with private choice." He goes on to say: "The latest attack involves a perversion of needed regulatory reform, transforming the necessary elimination of redundant or counterproductive regulatory policies into something different: a drive to pull the teeth from health, environmental, and consumer programs. This attack, best termed 'the immobilization of truth' after one of its leaders, seeks to smother the critical facilities of the American people in a blanket of sophistries."

Mr. Speth obviously forgot that he represents a federal agency concerned with the needs and rights of *all* people. His comments represent views similar to the NRDC, not the Chairman of CEQ, when he advises: "First we must keep doing, and keep doing better, those things that have already worked so well—educating, lobbying, suing, working within government at all levels."

The environmental leaders and their movement penetrated the Washington bureaucracy and achieved an effective power base. The federal acts and policies helped the environmental movement to achieve its land-use, air, and water goals at state and local levels; but not without a tremendous cost to the American economy.

Funding of the Environmental Movement

Finally, the growth of the environmental movement is attributable to enormous corporate funding. Environmental groups aren't funded entirely by membership dues and occasional contributions (as many would like to believe). The movement is big business, with major national contributors that include large foundations, corporations, and industrial oil company foundations.

In 1979 the Ford Foundation contributed $6,162,155 to environmental organizations; the Rockefeller Foundation, the Rockefeller Brothers Trust Fund, and the Rockefeller Family Fund contributed $9,519,296; the Stern Fund contributed $330,000; and the Atlantic Richfield Foundation contributed $7,768,955.

In California the annual state budgets for environmental causes are enormous, including: the Sierra Club ($1 million); the Natural Resources Defense Council ($500,000); and the Sierra Club Legal Defense Fund ($450,000). Thus the illusion of the environmental movement continues, a movement of citizens grass roots, led by affluent white professionals who live in enclaves for the rich, and funded by multimillion dollar contributions from corporate conglomerates.[36]

The environmental movement, led by elitists and funded by multi-million dollar grants has dramatically impacted the productivity of the American people, and in the process has converted a decent and necessary cause (the environment) into just another political movement and bureaucratic machine.

Chapter Five

Local Government Becomes a Victim

Cities, as well as private landowners, become victims of big-government plans, policies, and acquisition tactics.

Stearns Wharf Rehabilitation

Environmental agencies and their manipulation of regulations cost Santa Barbara and state taxpayers a considerable sum of money on the city's Stearns Wharf project. Most taxpayers in communities are not aware, unfortunately, of the hidden price they pay on projects similar to Stearns Wharf.

Santa Barbara's Stearns Wharf was constructed in 1872 by John Stearns as a municipal pier. In September of that year, when the steamer "Anne Stoffer" pulled up to the pier, Santa Barbara's first major communication link had been achieved. Operation of the pier continued until 1973 when a fire destroyed "The Harbor" restaurant. The unsafe condition of the wharf resulting from the fire caused it to be closed to the public. Until its closure in 1973, the wharf had flourished under private ownership, and at the date of the fire it boasted two restaurants, a bake shop, commercial fishing and related shops and facilities, and parking spaces actively used by the public.

Shortly after the fire, a private development company, The Old Santa Barbara Pier Company, in cooperation with the City of Santa Barbara, initiated plans for restoring the wharf. Their original proposal described a 90,000-square-foot commercial and retail development that included four restaurants, variety shops, and facilities supportive of commercial fishing. It was a total plan to convert the debris into a major recreational and tourist facility in the historic tradition of the pier.

In 1975 the Old Santa Barbara Pier Company and the City of Santa Barbara submitted their first proposal to the Coastal Commission. The regional commission approved the first proposal, but only after slashing the available commercial space to 60,000 square feet. The proposal failed, however, at the state commission level, and the Pier Company and City of Santa Barbara commenced their planning anew.

In 1977 a second proposal was submitted and accepted by the regional commission. The project included only 48,470 square feet of commercial structures and used only approximately 50 percent of the surface of the pier for restaurants, shops, and offices. This development, which the proponents considered to be the minimum necessary to achieve economical feasibility, dedicated approximately 80 percent of the total rentable space to public eating at four major restaurants, with 3,000 square feet of the area to be used for business related to commercial fishing, such as bait shops and fish markets. The City of Santa Barbara agreed to construct a 120-space parking lot on shore adjacent to the pier, thus freeing the wharf from auto congestion. The state coastal commission denied this second proposal on the grounds that the development would prejudice the ability of local government to prepare its local coastal program for future uses of the area. The proposal was denied on these grounds even though the local government (the City of Santa Barbara) had approved the project and was the project's coapplicant to the Coastal Commission.

The proposals for Stearns Wharf had been in conformity with the mandates and goals of the Coastal Act of 1976, which stated "Visitor-serving commercial recreational facilities (hotels, motels, restaurants, etc.) designed to enhance public opportunities for coastal recreation shall have priority over private residential, general industrial, or general commercial development. . . ." Nevertheless, the state coastal commission found grounds for declaring that this development would have a significant adverse impact on the environment "whereas feasible alternatives exist which would substantially reduce these adverse impacts."

In 1978, the City of Santa Barbara, owner of the property, terminated its lease with the Old Santa Barbara Pier Company, which had not been able to obtain a permit from the Coastal Commission to develop the property. The private project died and with it went a loss of over \$1 million in expenditures by the Pier Company (lease payments, pier restoration costs, development plans, etc.).

The "feasible alternatives" suggested by the Coastal Commission evolved in the form of the California Coastal Conservancy, a state government agency and sister agency of the Coastal Commission. The conservancy became the new proponent of its own development, and government assumed the role of private enterprise. The conservancy's proposal was a scaled-down version of the original proposals by the Old Santa Barbara Pier Company. Its plan included development of approximately 26,000 square feet and only two restaurants. This plan was accepted by the Coastal Commission. However, the Coastal Commission in a public release indicated that despite heavy subsidies (\$1.4 million from the Coastal Energy Impact Program, \$1 million from the City of Santa Barbara, \$400,000 from the Coastal Conservancy, and \$200,000 from the Wildlife Conservation Board), the project will operate at a loss. Present projections have this government project (not counting administrative costs) operating at a minimum \$71,000 to \$100,000 deficit per year.

The Coastal Commission had replaced a private, economically feasible project with a government-run, taxpayer-subsidized financial loss in order to avoid an alleged adverse impact on the environment, while stating that "more feasible alternatives" existed.

Monterey Urban Renewal

In 1969 owners of land in the city of Seaside, in Monterey County, California, began to proceed with plans for a four-acre hotel site on sand dunes on ocean-front property adjoining an existing Holiday Inn. Before those plans reached fruition, the City of Monterey engaged in discussions with the landowner and arrived at an arrangement by which several properties adjoining that beachfront ownership could be pooled into a community redevelopment project. This project would achieve an additional commercial recreational use through the erection of a much-needed hotel, in addition to providing open space, beach access, and beach frontage to the members of the public.

As a result of that activity, the owners of the property (James Bancroft and Michael Maloney) and the prospective tenant and builder of the hotel, Donald Lehman and Glasstree, Inc. entered into discussion with owners of adjoining property and the City of Monterey, leading to the formation of the Monterey Urban Renewal

Agency. Thereafter, that agency engaged in years of planning, financed by public and private contributors, which arrived at a master plan for development of the properties. That project, funded with a combination of $750,000 from matching federal funds and local community taxes, provided for a combination of uses: the construction of a 200-room luxury resort hotel in a depressed pocket of one of the properties and the creation of permanent open space and park facilities through public acquisition of the remaining properties.

In 1975-76 the City of Monterey, the Monterey Urban Renewal Agency, and the landowners jointly applied to the Coastal Commission for approval of this project, which was the culmination of years of mutual cooperation between local government, redevelopment agencies, and landowners. The regional and state coastal commissions denied the applications on the grounds that, instead of providing partial ownership of the property, the State of California should acquire all of the properties. That acquisition did not thereafter occur until the owners were forced to file an action for inverse condemnation and damages in 1978. Finally, in late 1979, after lengthy litigation and settlement discussions, the properties were acquired by the State of California for a price in excess of $4 million. The property is to be kept in its natural, unused condition.

The net effect of the Coastal Commission's action was to deny a community plan that would have created needed additional hotel units (stimulating the economy of a depressed neighborhood), public open space and beach area at little public cost, and a worthwhile redevelopment project. Instead, their action incurred a loss of $750,000 in matching federal funding and an additional cost of $3.5 million to the taxpayers, for no public or economic gain whatsoever, and for an ecological gain that would have been assured anyway by the project's open space program.

Usurpation of Local Government Planning

The passing of many federal acts inundated cities, counties, and other local government agencies with enormous amounts of paper work, extra planning, and a need for larger staffs. Federal and state environmental, resource, and planning legislation and directives had the effect of making local government officials the administrators of federal mandates, with little room for interpretation or flexible application. The traditional local planning process was soon riddled with new federal and state-mandated directives.

There are over 27 *federal* laws affecting *private land use.* Most of these laws impact local government and especially coastal communities. (The major federal acts affecting private land-use practices and their administering agencies, their purposes, and their effects are outlined in Figure 20 "Federal Laws Affecting Private Land Use Practices "[37].)

Traditional Community Planning Process

In the 1960s, in most states community planning was considered the art and science of preparing and administering within the framework of local government a long-range, comprehensive, and general plan for the physical development of the community. The goal of planning was to further the social and economic welfare of the people in a community and to create a more efficient and attractive community environment.

Planning was needed to prevent or solve problems created by: (1) population growth, which created a need for more and better housing and programs to remove deteriorated houses and buildings; (2) increased demands for public services such as water, sewerage, and parks; (3) increased public facility needs; (4) greater use of the automobile; (5) expanding residential areas; (6) a changing economic base; (7) rapidly rising taxes; and (8) changing agricultural patterns.

During the 1970s planning became more and more concerned with air quality, the environment, transportation, and energy, but land use regulations remained a key to controlling the environment.

The authority to plan at the local level was provided by legislation at the state level and ordinances at the county and city level. Legislation was locally passed that established a planning commission, a planning department, and rules and regulations under which they operated. General planning funds were sometimes obtained from federal housing and community development grants.

The "general plan" was the major vehicle used by communities for planning anticipated growth. It was usually a long-range, comprehensive, general guide to the growth of the community that was understandable, available, and amendable. The plan was concerned with all the needs of the citizens of a community in which the use of land was involved. All public and private land was included in the plan.

Figure 20:   Federal laws affecting private land use practices.

FEDERAL LAWS AFFECTING PRIVATE LAND USE PRACTICES

Name (citation)	Administering Agency	Primary Purpose	Land Use Effect
Natural Resource Laws			
National Environmental Policy Act (42 USC §4321 *et seq.*)	Council on Environmental Quality	Reduce the degradation of the human environment and achieve a balance between development and resource use.	Requires federal agencies and licensees to analyze impacts of actions on land and water resources and to choose the environmentally preferable alternative or to explain why that alternative was not chosen.
Land and Water Conservation Fund (16 USC §4601-5)	Heritage Conservation and Recreation Service	Provide financial incentives for state and local governments to provide recreation areas and opportunities.	Requires adoption of 5-year State Comprehensive Outdoor Recreation Plans to guide recreation land acquisition and development activities.
Coastal Zone Management Act (16 USC §1451 *et seq.*)	Office of Coastal Zone Management	Assist coastal and Great Lake states in preparing and implementing state coastal plans.	Requires states to adopt acceptable coastal plans as condition for continued federal assistance; plans generally designate permissible uses of coastal lands.

Law	Agency	Purpose	Description
Floodplain Management Executive Order (E.O. 11988)	Council on Environmental Quality, Water-Resources Council and Federal Emergency Management Administration	Reduce the risk of flood loss and restore or preserve natural floodplains.	Prohibits federal agencies and licensees from building in the 100-year floodplain unless there is no practicable alternative.
Protection of Wetlands Executive Order (E.O. 11990)	Council on Environmental Quality	Minimize the destruction of wetlands.	Requires federal agencies to avoid construction in wetlands unless there is no practicable alternative.
Fish and Wildlife Coordination Act (16 USC § 661 et seq.)	Fish and Wildlife Service	Ensure wildlife conservation needs receive agency consideration when water-related impacts will result from federal projects.	Fish and Wildlife Service and state wildlife agencies can recommend modifications of projects to reduce impacts on wildlife habitat.
Water Resources Planning Act (42 USC § 1962 et seq.)	Water Resources Council	Encourage the conservation, development, and utilization of water on a coordinated basis.	Establishes River Basin commissions to coordinate water and related land development; statewide water resource planning must be consistent with these planning policies.
Agricultural Marketing Agreement Act of 1973; Agricultural Adjustment Act of 1938 (7 USC § 601 et seq.) (7 USC § 1281 et seq.)	Agricultural Stabilization and Conservation Service	Stabilizes prices, markets, and farm incomes and conserves resources.	Affects land use and crop management practices through set-aside programs, acreage allotments, and marketing limitations and subsidies.
Consolidated Farm and Rural Development Act of 1961 (7 USC § 1921 et seq.)	Farmers Home Administration	Finance real estate, operating, and emergency loans for soil and water conservation and rural industrialization.	Provides money for watershed and erosion protection, flood prevention, and soil and water projects.

Name (citation)	Administering Agency	Primary Purpose	Land Use Effect
Natural Resource Laws			
Surface Mining Control and Reclamation Act of 1977 (30 USC § 1201 *et seq.*)	Office of Surface Mining	Protect society and environment from adverse effects of surface coal mining.	Regulates surface mining on both private and public lands and prohibits mining on critical lands.
Marine Protection, Research, and Sanctuaries Act of 1972 (16 USC 1431–1434)	Office of Coastal Zone Management	Designate marine areas as sanctuaries for conservation, recreation, or ecological purposes.	Allows only activities compatible with marine sanctuaries protection to be conducted within sanctuary boundaries.
Endangered Species Act of 1973 (16 USC § 1531 *et seq.*)	Fish and Wildlife Service	Conserve ecosystems for the use of endangered or threatened species.	Requires that federal agency actions anticipate threats to and be consistent with survival of endangered and threatened species and their critical habitats, whether or not the area is designated as critical habitat.
Watershed Protection and Flood Prevention (16 USC § 1001 *et seq.*)	Soil Conservation Service	Prevent floods, conserve and utilize water and land resources.	Helps local organizations plan for community development and forecast demands for residential, commercial, industrial and recreational facilities in a comprehensive manner.

Name (citation)	Administering Agency	Primary Purpose	Land Use Effect
Community Development Laws			
Housing and Community Development Act of 1974 (42 USC § 5301)	Department of Housing and Urban Development	Encourage comprehensive planning for the development of human and natural resources by state, region.	Provides grants for the planning and development of community facilities and services such as housing projects and recreation.
National Flood Insurance Act of 1968 (42 USC § 4001)	Federal Emergency Management Administration	Reduce the risk of loss due to flooding.	Requires designated flood-prone communities to develop flood mitigation measures including land use, elevation and building requirements as a condition for flood insurance coverage.
Disaster Relief Act (42 USC § 5121)	Federal Emergency Management Administration	Mitigate losses from disasters and provide emergency assistance for major natural disasters.	Requires state and local governments to adopt measures which may discourage building on hazard-prone lands.
National Historic Preservation Act (16 USC § 470 et seq.)	Advisory Council on Historic Preservation	Protect districts, buildings, sites and objects significant to American history.	Requires that federal agency actions consider impacts of their actions on property registered in or eligible for the National Historic Register.
Federal-Aid Highway Act (23 USC § 101 et seq.)	Federal Highway Administration	Develop state and interstate highway system.	Provides grants to states for the construction of highway systems.

Name (citation)	Administering Agency	Primary Purpose	Land Use Effect
Community Development Laws			
Urban Mass Transit Act of 1964 (49 USC § 1601 *et seq.*)	Urban Mass Transit Administration	Encourage the reconstruction and expansion of urban transit systems.	Provides grants to urban areas for public transportation.
Public Works and Economic Development (42 USC § 3121 *et seq.*)	Economic Development Administration	Stimulate community development through a wide range of subsidized community projects.	Provides grants to communities to develop facilities such as public works and roads.
Water Resources Development Act of 1974 (33 USC § 701 *et seq.*)	Army Corps of Engineers	Reduce the loss of life and property due to floods through dam and reservoir projects.	Provides for the construction of dams and reservoirs to reduce uncontrolled flooding and provide recreational benefits.
Pollution Control Laws			
Clean Water Act (33 USC § 1251 *et seq.*)	Environmental Protection Agency; U.S. Army Corps of Engineers	Reduce water pollution and the discharge of toxic and waste materials into all waters.	Makes grants for sewage treatment plants, which may encourage or permit growth; requires state to regulate land use practices to control pollution from indirect (non-point) sources such as urban areas; requires wetland concerns to be considered in U.S. Army Corps of Engineers dredge and fill permits.

Act	Agency	Purpose	Requirements
Safe Drinking Water Act (42 USC § 300 (F))	Environmental Protection Agency	Assure public is provided safe drinking water.	Permits Environmental Protection Agency to veto federal agency and licensee projects that could contaminate the watershed of a municipality's only source of drinking water.
Clean Air Act (42 USC § 1857 *et seq.*)	Environmental Protection Agency	Reduce air pollution dangerous to public health, crops, livestock, and property.	Limits development in pristine areas, and affects siting of new industrial facilities in all areas.
Resource Conservation and Recovery Act of 1976 (42 USC § 6901 *et seq.*)	Environmental Protection Agency	Control of waste disposal and hazardous wastes.	Requires that all solid wastes, other than hazardous wastes be disposed of in sanitary landfill or utilized for resource recovery.
Rivers and Harbors Act of 1899 (33 USC § 401 *et seq.*)	Army Corps of Engineers	Protect navigation, water quality, fish and wildlife, ecology, and aesthetics of navigable waters.	Requires that effects on wildlife habitat, wetlands, historic resources, and coastal zones be considered before granting a permit for activities in navigable waters.
Deepwater Port Act of 1974 (33 USC § 1501 *et seq.*)	United States Coast Guard	Regulate the construction and operation of deepwater ports on the seas to transfer oil from tankers to shore.	Requires land-based development effects to be considered in any port license and be consistent with state environmental laws or coastal zone programs.

Planning Commissions

Planning commissions, appointed by city councils or boards of supervisors, generally served in an advisory capacity to the city council or board of supervisors on planning matters. Usually, the commission would hold public hearings and make recommendations to the council or board on general and specific plans prepared by the staff concerning land development. The commissions often held public hearings on zone-change applications, subdivisions, and amendments to the various elements of the general plan such as land-use, circulation, and community facilities. The council and board of supervisors adopted plans, amendments, and zone changes after receiving recommendations from the planning commission.

Planning Departments

Planning departments were usually responsible for providing technical advice to the planning commission and the city council or board of supervisors and for making recommendations to them on planning and zoning matters. The department was often responsible for preparing and administering a general plan for the physical development of the community, guided by the policies established by the legislative branch. Planners trained in physical planning and research usually prepared the general and specific plans. In preparing plans, the planning staffs tended to work closely with city, county, and state departments, private companies, and citizens.

This planning development also was often responsible for conducting research on planning, preparing subdivision and zoning regulations, administering subdivision and zoning regulations, and participating in capital improvement programming. It also cooperated with cities within a county, with nearby counties, and with state and federal agencies in developing a plan for the community that related with the regional plans of the area.

General Plans

The contents of most general plans included considerations for:

1. Population characteristics growth
2. Land use
3. Community facilities
4. Circulation system
5. Urban design

General plans were usually brought into reality, or implemented, by a variety of planning tools.

Zoning maps and regulations were the legislative instruments for controlling land with respect to use, population, density, location, lot size, the density and placement of buildings, and heights of structures.

Subdivision ordinances regulated how land was to be subdivided for various uses. It was a major tool for achieving a desirable physical environment.

Capital improvement programs outlined in two- to six-year programs the amount of funds needed to attain part of the community facilities outlined in the general plan. These included items such as water, sewer and flood control facilities, schools, courts, and government buildings.

Community renewal programs were specific projects prepared for improving and reviewing deteriorating and substandard neighborhoods and community areas and preventing their demise into slums. Federal funds were frequently provided to cities for urban renewal and housing projects.

"Staging of development for growth location" programs anticipated growth and staged it to guide the extension and construction of public streets and community facilities and private facilities in an orderly and economic manner.

How Traditional Planning Changed

With the development of federal and state-mandated programs in the 1970s, new requirements, regulations, and controls made rapid changes in this general local planning structure. The new legislation programs had an impact on the land-use regulations for development throughout the country, including: (1) the location, type of use, densities, and standards of development; (2) growth management; and (3) transportation networks such as roads, public transportation, airports and harbors.

The new legislation also had an impact on location, standards, and timing of construction for water, sewer, flood control, highway, and other capital improvements involved in federal programs.

The requirement for preparing environmental impact reports for all public and private projects having a possible impact on the environment changed local planning throughout the whole nation, perhaps the most in California.

With so many agencies directly or indirectly regulating local environment, private property, and development, the rights of property owners are often violated. Arbitrary decisions by agencies controlling water and sewer line expansion, Air Pollution Control District regulations, and other development and programs, strongly affected the local property values, investments, and the cost of housing projects. In many cases, property owners became caught between different agencies administering conflicting regulations for the same area, with each agency refusing to relinquish its control to the other.

In general, federal environmental regulations had their greatest local impact on land use, air quality control, population control, water and sewer systems, and growth control programs. Planning authority and control by local agencies were eroded by these actions. Communities tried different approaches to cope with the various mandated programs, but were frustrated for the following reasons:

1. Federal and state governments expect local and regional agencies to implement their programs, but they retain direct or indirect authority to implement all or parts of the clean air, clean water, and transportation plans. Local government is put in the untenable position of having responsibility without authority.
2. More than one federal or state agency have authority to implement or operate programs locally through allocation of powers among local jurisdictions, overlapping jurisdictions or have "overriding" authority.
3. Regionalization of authority through creation of federal and/or state-mandated single-purpose agencies gives the agencies the authority to override or block local land-use decisions.

Ventura County: A Case Study in Coordinating Federal Mandates

Most cities and counties absorbed the mandated programs within existing departments or merged various departments and their new functions into "environmental resource" type agencies. Officials were aware that staffs and costs mounted rapidly as a result, but these costs were not easily identified.

One coastal county in California, in an attempt to coordinate the various federal programs and planning mandates, took a different approach to the situation. As a result, some of the planning costs attributed to federally imposed programs could be identified. Ventura County's case history illustrates what happened throughout the country, but in a more fragmented fashion and hidden from easy identification.

110

Ventura County is 1,851 square miles and is located along the coast about 50 miles north of the city of Los Angeles. In 1980 it had a population of about 525,000.

The federal aid and subsidies offered for planning and construction for various programs looked attractive in the 1970s. After spending years on local planning, the communities learned they had to change their plans to meet federal mandates.

Regional Land-Use Program

Several Ventura public agency officials thought that a coordinated planning approach might be the best method of meeting the federal and state mandates. As Section 208 of the Federal Water Pollution Control Act of 1972 required countywide planning, but also made funding available to improve water quality, a regional planning process was established. Likewise, four separate countywide programs, called the Regional Land Use Program (RLUP), later called the Countywide Planning Program, were established. The programs coordinated together were:

Program	Lead Agency
208 Areawide Waste Treatment Management Plan	Ventura Regional County Sanitation District (VRCSD)
Air Quality Maintenance Plan	Air Pollution Control District (APCD)
Spheres of Influence Plan	Local Agency Formation Commission (LAFCO)
Subregional Transportation Plan	Ventura County Association of Governments (VCAG)

The Ventura County Regional Sanitation District was designated by California Governor Jerry Brown in 1974 as the most appropriate organization to function in the lead role for development of the initial "208" Plan in California. The planning effort was funded initially for two years with a grant of $918,000.

As shown in Figure 21, "1975–78 Regional Land Use Program Structure," an elaborate organization was established to coordinate the planning effort among Ventura County, the nine cities within the county, and various regional agencies involved. Keep in mind that this complicated organization was an addition to the existing planning agencies.

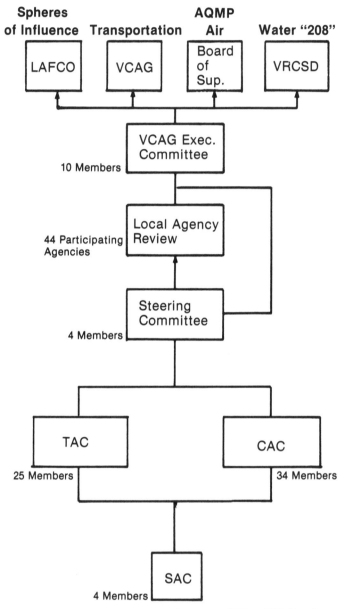

Figure 21: Ventura County, California, 1975–1978 Regional Land Use Program (RLUP) structure.

The Ventura Regional County Sanitation District (VRCSD) contracted agreements for planning services from many of the agencies expected to implement the plans. The Air Quality Maintenance and 208 Waste Water Management Programs required the development and implementation of a "comprehensive regional land-use plan" that would control the type and location of land uses in order to minimize the adverse effects on air and water quality.

A required transportation study and sphere-of-influence study were also incorporated as they involved land-use considerations, 1990 population forecasts, and ultimate geographical service area boundaries. It was decided that close coordination with these programs would be logical and advantageous in developing additional population and land-use forecasts. The participating agencies reasoned that the objective of collecting data required by all four programs could be served better by a comprehensive and coordinated program.

The purpose of the RLUP process was to analyze and integrate common planning elements of the individual federally-mandated program areas of transportation, waste water management (208), air quality maintenance, and spheres of influence.

A special planning staff was established along with a Staff Advisory Committee (SAC) consisting of the chief staff officer of each of the four major planning agencies involved in the program. To insure that federal requirements for citizen involvement were adequate, a Citizens' Advisory Committee (CAC) was created, composed of representatives of a variety of geographic, economic, political, social, and environmental interests. The CAC met at least once a month for a 2½ year period. To insure adequate technical participation, a Technical Advisory Committee (TAC) was formed. It included representatives of all nine cities, the four participating agencies, selected special districts, and county and extra-county entities.

To provide policy-level contact between the Regional Land Use Program and the respective participating agencies, a Regional Land Use Program Steering Committee was established, consisting of an elected official from each of the policy boards responsible for the four regional planning products.

Recommendations of participants were forwarded to the Ventura County Association of Governments (VCAG) Executive Committee. The executive committee was composed of one representative from each of the nine cities and the county. The executive committee acted upon all plans and recommendations prior to the final submittal to the forty-four local agencies for their final action. This included the nine cities, the County of Ventura, APCD, LAFCO, VRCSD, VCAG, citizens' groups, and other organizations.

Citizen Participation in Planning

The Ventura Regional County Sanitation District (VRCSD) was, in addition, advised by a forty-member Areawide Planning Advisory Committee (APAC). APAC consisted of technicians and citizens from a variety of public and private local agencies and selected state and regional agencies. Several other advisory committees were formed to assist in the RLUP planning process. The advisory committees made recommendations to the policy boards as well as to the RLUP Steering Committee.

Many public hearings were held to review the various recommendations and policies evolving from the program. Other newsletters, questionnaires, and brochures were sent out by the staff during the planning process. All this staff work and hearings were in addition to the regular planning and EIR process.

The final product of the 208 Areawide Waste Treatment Management Plan consisted of a plan in report form, including maps and charts that identified problem areas, areawide goals, alternative control measures for population, and a final plan including land-use, water quality, and air quality, an implementation plan, and continuing planning program. The land-use portion established geographic expansion limits for cities to the year 1990 and 2000. The plan set growth limits, a *maximum* for population growth, and the general location of land uses. In the water quality section, the goals and plans for upgrading the quality of water and waste water treatment were described. In the air quality section, land-use and population limits were established to insure that the National Ambient Air Quality Standards (NAAQS) be obtained on schedule.

To achieve the NAAQS standard and to adhere to the mandates and policies of the various acts, a reduced population forecast and land-use expansion for most of the cities and the county emerged. This caused great anger and controversy among the city councils, builders, labor unions, and agency officials. The employees of cities had spent considerable time and money and held many public hearings over several years completing and adopting their own general plan. The establishment of new, smaller population forecasts and restricted urbanization area as a result of federal and state intervention was upsetting to investors, home builders, and some public agencies, alike.

They had planned their activities and budgets for years according to previous legally adopted plans. The standards set for some communities were so harsh that the existing populations were equal to the forecasts and permitted population for 1990 and 2000.

The People Bank

As a result of the plan, the County Board of Supervisors established a "people bank." If a builder or individual desired to build a house in an area where the future population was already committed, he had to make a formal application to the board of supervisors to draw needed "bodies" from a "people bank." One dwelling unit was permitted three "bodies." Only after the board of supervisors granted a builder permission to take "bodies" from the "people bank" could he get his building permit.

Participating agencies and cities were very concerned with the RLUP study because of the unfair hardships placed on them. Cities had sized their sewer and water system and capital improvement programs for a much larger population than had been approved in the RLUP program. Their planning efforts had been wasted. When the study was initiated, the cities did not take it seriously. It seemed like just "another study." Too late, they found themselves boxed into a rigid population formula and land-use forecasts based on federal and state standards.

At a public hearing before the board of supervisors, one of the supervisors indicated that he had measured the height of the reports and studies completed by the RLUP staff over a two and a half year period. They measured seven feet high. The audience's groaning response indicated that they were familiar with the superfluous quantity of data that poured out of the staff.

Upon the adoption of the 208 Areawide Waste Treatment Management Plan, participants anticipated that the study would end and the expensive staff operations would be disbanded. To their dismay, however, they found a proposal from the staff stating that federal and state mandates required the program to continue. It was necessary to revise the population and land-use plan already completed to comply with federal mandates. A budget was recommended for the next two years (1978–1980) of about $1,887,600. Seventy-five percent came from federal funding, which meant that taxpayers in other states contributed to the program. Most of the work proposed in the new study was updating type work.

115

RLUP Costs to Ventura County

The RLUP and countywide program, from December 1975 through July 1981, was budgeted for $3,354,400. The cities' and the county planning departments, in a three-year period (1976–1979), spend $7,901,513 on planning, in addition to the RLUP budget. This did not include money spent in Ventura County on planning by the Regional Coastal Commission, SCAG (Southern California Association of Governments), SCAT (the transportation system for Ventura county), the National Park Service, State Park Service, special districts such as water and sewer systems, and many other agencies.

Figure 22, "Major Federal, State and Regional Agencies/Programs Impacting Local Planning Powers in Ventura County," shows the impact of federal, state, and regional agency policies on local planning powers. This costly impact on local government is occuring throughout the United States but usually in a less identifiable manner. (See Appendix B for descriptions of acts and agencies impacting the city and county governments in Ventura.)

The RLUP program established new layers of government and a staff without clear lines of authority to anyone. Not only was the RLUP effort a duplication of existing city and agency planning, but there is doubt that it made any improvement in the environment or quality of life for people in the county.

Federal Agencies		Land Use	Population Control	Environmental Protection	Housing	Pollution Control	Air	Water	Flood Control	Energy	Transportation	Harbors	Airports
EPA	Environmental Protection Agency	•	•	•	•	•	•	•	•	•	•	•	•
HUD	Housing & Urban Development	•	•	•	•					•			
DOT	Dept. of Transportation	•	•		•		•		•	•	•	•	•
DOE	Dept. of Energy	•	•	•	•	•	•	•		•	•	•	•
FOCZM	Federal Office of Coastal Zone Management	•	•	•	•	•	•	•		•	•	•	•
DOI	Dept. of Interior	•											
PUC	Public Utility Commission	•	•	•	•	•				•			
State Agencies		•	•	•									
OPR	Office of Planning Research	•	•	•	•	•					•		
DH	Dept. of Housing	•	•	•	•	•					•		
CEQA	California Environmental Quality Agency	•	•	•	•	•	•	•	•	•	•	•	•
CCC	California Coastal Commission	•	•	•	•	•	•	•	•	•	•	•	•
ARB	Air Resources Board	•	•	•	•	•	•	•			•	•	•
WRB	Water Resources Board	•	•	•	•	•		•	•	•			
SWMB	Solid Waste Management Board	•		•	•	•	•				•		
Caltrans		•	•	•	•		•			•	•		•
CSRA	California State Resources Agency	•	•	•	•	•				•			
DH	Dept. of Health												
SF & G	State Fish & Game			•		•		•	•				
Regional Agencies													
LAFCO	Local Agency Formation Control Commission	•	•		•	•	•	•		•	•		
APCD	Air Pollution Control District	•	•	•	•	•	•			•	•		
SCAG	Southern California Association of Governments	•	•	•	•	•	•	•	•	•	•	•	•
VCAG	Ventura County Association of Governments	•	•	•	•	•	•				•	•	•
RCC	Regional Coastal Commission	•	•	•	•	•	•	•	•	•	•	•	•
RWQCB	Regional Water Quality Control Board	•	•	•	•	•	•	•	•	•	•	•	•
VRCSD	Ventura Regional County Sanitation District	•	•	•	•	•		•	•	•			
Special Districts		•	•	•	•	•			•	•		•	•

Figure 22: Major federal, state, and regional agencies impacting local planning powers in Ventura County, California.

Chapter Six

Never In America

The environmental movement has dramatically altered our concept of individual liberty. In many instances, the destruction of constitutional protections has been justified as a necessary effect of "state" goals. That erosion of individual rights, the violations of due process, and in a final sense, the taking of property by government are events without historic parallel in this country. Commonplace and occasionally institutionalized in foreign countries, these events are an anathema to our nation, which is predicated upon a unique system of checks and balances and a constitutional guarantee that our judicial system will protect and defend individual rights against the encroachment of government excesses.

The history of our constitutional law is rooted in a concept of the sanctity of private property and its protection in an American state and federal court system, a history that evolved from the concern manifested in the American revolution. On July 4, 1776, when a group of disorganized American colonies announced their independence, they did so in the spirit of the inalienable rights of John Locke and the freedoms of Adam Smith, a declaration that "all men are created equal, they are endowed by their Creator with certain inalienable rights, that among these are life, liberty, and the pursuit of happiness." However, initially, that phrase was not without controversy. As Alistair Cooke would explain nearly two centuries later:

> There was a lot of argument among the States over the phrase.
> And in the end many of the men who signed the Declaration,
> while letting "happiness" stand as a no doubt worthy general

Photo 1: Earth-covered homes in Otter Cove, California.

Photo 2: Earth-covered homes in Otter Cove, California.

Photo 3: Home in Cuyahoga Valley slated for demolition.
Courtesy of the National Inholders Association

Photo 4: Home in Cuyahoga Valley slated for demolition.

Courtesy of the National Inholders Association

Photo 5: Home under demolition in Cuyahoga Valley.
Courtesy of the National Inholders Association

Photo 6: Home under demolition in Cuyahoga Valley.

Courtesy of the National Inholders Association

Photo 7: Home under demolition in Cuyahoga Valley.
Courtesy of the National Inholders Association

Photo 8: Cannery Row, Monterey, California.

Photo 9: Spindrift Hotel, Cannery Row, Monterey, California.

Photo 10: Cannery Row, Monterey, California.

Photo 11: Cannery Row, Monterey, California.

Photo 12: Cannery Row, Monterey, California.

Photo 13: Cannery Row, Monterey, California.

Photo 14: Harborplace, James Rouse's New Baltimore Inner-harbor Project.

Photo 15: Harborplace, James Rouse's New Baltimore Inner-harbor Project.

Photo 16: Harborplace, James Rouse's New Baltimore
Inner-harbor Project.

Photo 17: Mussel Shoals beach homes and the controversial rocks.

Photo 18: Mussel Shoals beach homes and the controversial rocks.

Photo 19: Marina Dunes development site.

Photo 20: Stearns Wharf, Santa Barbara, California.

Photo 21: Stearns Wharf, Santa Barbara, California.

Photo 22: The Briggs's property near adjacent subdivision.

"They made us many promises, more than I can remember,
but they never kept but one;
they promised to take our land, and they took it."

(Tatanka Yotanka)

Sitting Bull

Photo 23: Chief Sitting Bull.   Artist: Jack Pardue

aim, went home and wrote into their separate State constitutions
"life, liberty, and the pursuit of property." This was not merely a
tycoon's reflex. To most of them, property was no dowry. It was
the means of life they, or their fathers or grandfathers, had been
forced to wrench out of a wilderness.[38]

In essence, the acquisition and protection of private property
reflected the earned liberty of an entire generation and the basis in
great part for the independence of the American Colonial states.

This notion of private property rights and the earned liberties of
property owners was an evolutionary notion imposed after centuries
of philosophical debate of the basis of property ownership and the
right to its distribution and use. Through this evolution emerged a
constitutional right of private property guaranteed by an independent
American judicial system.

The world has developed into a chasm of two distinct and com-
peting economic philosophies: private property ownership versus
government ownership, as in a very general sense found in the com-
peting philosophies of John Locke and Karl Marx.

A plethora of historic works has been devoted to the theories and
principles of Karl Marx: the conflicting and changing forces of
history, denominated "dialectic materialism,"[39] the prophesized
ultimate class struggle (workers v. wealthy) establishing a temporary
dictatorship of the proletariat (working class), and the control and use
in common of the means and products of production.

The dogma of Marx has never realized its implementation in a
true communist state. Marxism lives as a theoretical goal of those socialist nations that maintain government control of property rather
than classless communal ownership of property. However, the ultimate communist state envisions the elimination of private property:

> In this sense, the theory of the communists may be summed up in
> a single sentence: abolition of private property. . . . In one word,
> you reproach us with intending to do away with your property.
> Precisely so; that is just what we intended.[40]

Of greater significance, and in frightening detail, the *Communist
Manifesto* outlined a series of sequential steps toward the elimination
of the capitalistic state through abolition of private property. Most of
those steps involved an attack upon the right of ownership and use of
property and attendant labor and work. Among its many goals, the

Communist Manifesto predicted "abolition of property and land and application of all rents of land to public purposes"; "abolition of all right of inheritance"; "confiscation of the property of all immigrants and rebels"; and then a series of steps by which the control of credit and capital, factories and instruments of production, means of communication and transportation, would all be centralized.

The antithesis to the communal society is reflected in the movement of liberalism,[41] as espoused by John Locke (1632–1704). His core philosophy was that the singular purpose of government was to protect the right to "life, liberty, and property." Locke concluded that property was the greatest of these rights, in that it represented the earned result of one's labor: earned liberty.[42]

The concept of "earned liberty" evolved to a nation of laissez faire (complete governmental noninterference with business) and the intrinsic value of the individual profit motive.

In *Wealth of Nations* (1776) Adam Smith argued that the marketplace and the reality of supply and demand, unregulated by government interference, would better serve society than government-mandated goals.

The American Revolution reflected a nation's own demand for economic independence from foreign dominance. Twelve years later, at the first session of the American Congress, the Bill of Rights mandated individual freedoms, with a specific guarantee for the sanctity of private property ownership from uncompensated interference by government: ". . . nor [shall any person] be deprived of life, liberty or property without due process of law; nor shall private property be taken for public use without just compensation."[43]

This constitutional guarantee became the foundation for subsequent judicial restraints against government conduct which violated individual rights. The American judicial system became the guarantor of private property ownership, a fundamental right created in the American Revolution.

Over the next two centuries our judiciary reinforced this right, while serving as a buffer between unreasonable government regulation and individual rights. Although numerous judicial decisions tested this guarantee against a variety of government regulations, the principle remained basically intact. The American Constitution guaranteed individual property rights against unreasonable government regulation.

In 1922 Supreme Court Justice Oliver Wendell Holmes confirmed this constitutional guarantee. "The general rule at least is, that while property may be regulated to a certain extent, if regulation goes too far it will be recognized as a taking."[44] The complexity of American life, and the growing involvement of government in land-use regulation caused a myriad of challenges to that guarantee. In many instances government intrusions into private property rights were upheld, in others invalidated. But in each instance the test remained the same.

In 1972 the United States Supreme Court again confirmed the guarantee in "*Lynch* v. *Household Finance Corporation*" (1972) 405 U.S. 535,552:

> Property does not have rights, people have rights. The right to enjoy property without unlawful deprivation, no less than the right to speak or the right to travel, is in truth a personal right, whether the property in question be a welfare check, a home, or a savings account. In fact, fundamental interdependence exists between the personal right to liberty and the personal right to property. Neither can have meaning without the other.

The same guarantee has been rooted in each of our state courts, such as California's:

> The right of acquiring, possessing, and protecting property is anchored in the First Section of the First Article of our constitution. This right is as old as Magna Charta. It lies at the foundation of our constitutional government and is necessary to the existence of civil liberty and free institutions.[45]

Moreover, the California Supreme Court once recognized that "it is a principle of universal law that wherever the right to own property is recognized in the free government, practically all other rights become worthless if the government possesses an uncontrollable power over the property of the citizen."[46]

The Fifth Amendment to our constitution guarantees two primary liberties: that a citizen is entitled to "due process" of law, and that the government may not take a citizen's property without payment of just compensation.

The Anglo-American concept of due process basically stands for the proposition that a citizen is entitled to a system of fair hearings. Paramount to that system is an impartial judge, an opportunity to be heard, and a confrontation with the opposition—in essence, that an individual be given the fullest and fairest hearing in which to present his factual position, with knowledge of the identity and representations of his opposition, and with opportunity to cross-examine and fully explore the merits of the opposition.

The concept of just compensation for the taking of property by government is far more complex. Initially, this guarantee concerned the government's formal acquisition of a legal proceeding known as eminent domain (also known as direct condemnation). By this proceeding, the government acquires ownership of private property holdings for such public uses (highways, government buildings, parks) after paying the owner just compensation, which is usually defined as the fair market value of the property.

Normally, this process is initiated after public hearings and legislative determination that public acquisition is necessary for the public good. Thereafter the acquisition occurs either through negotiated purchase or court action in which a judge or jury determines the fair market value of the property. Once the court award of just compensation is paid to the owner, the government assumes title, possession and responsibility for the property.

Inverse Condemnation

This constitutional guarantee also applies to those instances in which constitutional rights to property have been violated, or indeed destroyed, but for which no compensation has been paid to the landowner. In these instances, the property owner's remedy is usually an action entitled "inverse condemnation" by which he sues his government and seeks an award of just compensation for the resulting injuries and damages he has sustained. If the owner prevails by convincing the court that his constitutional property rights have been violated, then the court awards "just compensation," and may direct the government to assume control and ownership of the land it has injured. Historically, this theory of "inverse condemnation" has allowed a citizen to enforce his own constitutional protections against a recalcitrant government.

The field of inverse condemnation harbors three primary theories of judicial acceptance. First, government may be held liable for physical trespass invasions of private property that substantially interfere with or impair its use. Trespass cases involve government conduct that deprives an owner of access to property or impairs its use, such as flooding, or injures its enjoyment, such as aircraft overflights. In these instances the government must compensate the owner for damages but does not necessarily assume ownership of the property.

Second, the courts have awarded compensation in those instances in which a government regulation is so excessive, arbitrary or unreasonable as to constitute a "de facto" taking or economic confiscation of property. This type of "inverse" action typically arises in instances in which a government has imposed unreasonably excessive regulations. For example, if a property previously zoned for one dwelling unit per acre is downzoned to one dwelling unit per 400 acres, this action severely if not totally devalues the subject property. In another example, a government may restrict the use of the property to one which is not economically or practically possible (i.e., restricting land with depleted soils and insufficient water to agricultural uses).

The third main theory of inverse condemnation involves often subtle and conspiratorial instances where government has deceived or violated the condemnation process. In these cases, a government may have intended or planned to acquire properties through eminent domain and payment of compensation, but devised subtle methods of preventing use of that property through regulation without compensation. This would arise when a government has determined to acquire a specific piece of property for public use as a park (open space), but then decided that the same open space could be created through preventing development of the property. This conduct reflects a conscious decision by a government entity to achieve public use (open space vistas) through regulations designed to prevent use of the property without payment of compensation.

The principle that regulatory power may not be used to subvert the constitutional guarantee of payment of just compensation has been applied in a uniform manner in both federal and state courts. In federal courts, members of the judiciary decried the conduct of the City of Palo Alto. This affluent residential community along the San Francisco Peninsula, initiated efforts to acquire private lands for public use, but instead implemented as an alternative, excessive downzoning of all property to an unreasonable low density. The city thus obtained its desired state of open space without paying a dollar of just compensation.[47]

In California state courts, the same principle has been applied in recognition that if "use or enjoyment of his [a person's] land was in any degree abridged or destroyed by reasons of the power of eminent domain, his property is *pro tanto* taken and he is entitled to compensation."[48]

Within this context of federal protections, the right to due process and the constitutional guarantees of just compensation, came the environmental movement.

In the name of the environment, a series of extraordinary tests of this constitutional guarantee were launched. Those tests would determine whether state or government goals could usurp individual rights. The paramount testing ground became the California court system.

Judicial Support of Environmental Movement

In February 1979 an analysis of recent legal decisions by Los Angeles attorney Michael Burger disclosed that the California judicial system had virtually endorsed all conduct of the California Coastal Commission engineered in the name of the environment. By that date the commission had participated in thirty-two decisions (appellate) challenging the commission's conduct and survived with a success rate of 87.5 percent, including a more astounding success record of 88.9 percent reversals of its own losses before trial courts.[49]

The Coastal Commission, through advocacy of public policy and environmental goals, had achieved a 90 percent victory rate in the appellate courts reversing its own losses in trial courts. The abuses of the California Coastal Commission had been condoned by the court system in the name of the environment.

Soon the courts found that "the agency's action comes before the court with a presumption of correctness and regularity" regardless of any findings to the contrary by a lower trial court.[50] They held that any citizen and resident of California would have standing to oppose a permit application or to appeal a permit approval to the State Commission, whether or not that person had any interest at all in the property or the Coastal Commission,[51] an open invitation to every member of, for example, the Sierra Club or the Wilderness Society. The court allowed commissioners to vote on projects despite their having missed earlier hearings and evidence on that same application. The court described the practice as a "technical" violation which resulted in the absent members missing "some rhetoric."

Despite these and other numerous instances in which the procedural irregularities of the Coastal Commission have been blessed,[52] of greater concern were the instances of substantial injury and harm occasioned by the outright restriction of the use and development of property holdings. As noted in "Save the Coast," the Coastal Commission had created without authorization or funding its own list of private property holdings that should be acquired by the State of

California. Historically, the state and federal courts would have mandated an award of compensation through the theory of inverse condemnation on any one of the last two theories discussed herein (confiscation or prelude cases). But in the name of the environment, the ban on use and development of property without an award of compensation allowed the denigration of the Constitution.

The *Briggs* Case

No appellate decision reflects as vividly the court system's blind acceptance of constitutional violations by a government agency as the Briggs case.[53] No other single set of facts illustrates as well such a blatant disregard of constitutional rights, interference by collaborating government agencies to destroy property rights, or disregard by appellate courts of the constitutional indignities. The Briggs decision represented the first significant victory over the Coastal Commission. Moreover it demonstrated the extent to which the government combined all the resources of a state to defeat the claims of one Mrs. Mitzi S. Briggs.

In 1963 Mrs. Briggs purchased approximately thirty-six acres of undeveloped oceanfront land located in the Carmel area overlooking the famed Point Lobos State Park. The property was bound on the north by residential development, on the east by historic Highway 1, and on the south by an additional state beach known as Monastery Beach. It was one of the last privately owned vestiges of beautiful beach-front property in Monterey County, California. The attractive property was of substantial value, having been purchased ten years earlier for over $1 million.

In 1972 Briggs obtained building permit approvals from the County of Monterey for the construction of three single-family residences on the 36-acre property. Within a month, the commission staff had completed its summary and recommended that the Coastal Commission approve the Briggs project. The staff noted that the project was consistent with the Coastal Act guidelines and would not have any substantial adverse environmental or ecological impact.

Prior to the public hearing, however, and unbeknownst to Briggs, a series of communications were exchanged between the Coastal Commission and officials of the State Department of Parks and Recreation. Soon thereafter in early May 1973, William Penn Mott, the Director of Parks and Recreation, telegrammed a Coastal Commissioner to confirm the State of California's interest in acquiring the

Briggs property. The Coastal Commission received additional correspondence from various officials of the Department of Parks and Recreation announcing the department's concern over any proposed development of the Briggs property.

On June 18, 1973 the Coastal Commission denied Briggs' application for development, finding that the proposed development "will have a substantial adverse environmental and ecological effect," a finding completely contrary to the earlier staff analysis, prior to nondisclosed communications.

Within a day, the commission had communicated to adjoining landowners the information that the Briggs application had been denied because of the interests of the Department of Parks and Recreation in acquiring the property as an adjunct to the Carmel River State Beach Park. Briggs later received a denial from the State Coastal Commission for the same reason and stating that development and use of her property would be prohibited.

The communications between staffs continued, even after the denial, all confirming the state's intent to acquire the Briggs property. This activity culminated in a meeting during which the director of California's parks and recreation department assured Mrs. Briggs that if she would forestall any further development, the acquisition would become a reality if a state parks bond issue passed.

When the State Beach Park Recreation and Historic Facilities Bond Act of 1974 passed, the State Park and Recreation Commission adopted a resolution recommending the acquisition of the Briggs property for the Carmel River State Beach.

In the interim, the Briggs property had been rendered valueless and unmarketable. Its value was dependent upon development. Mrs. Briggs twirled in a limbo, without property use, development, or income. Attempts were made by Briggs' representatives and attorneys to market and sell the property without any success. In fact, Briggs was unable even to obtain a brokerage listing.

In September of 1974 the governor of California signed an authorization for $1,750,000 for the acquisition of the Briggs property, yet the acquisition did not follow. The state government had, in effect, acquired without payment the exact use anticipated for the Briggs property: nonuse and open space.

On August 2, 1975 Briggs was compelled to file an inverse condemnation action against the State of California. She alleged that her property had been precluded from use and development as a result of planned public acquisition that had not occurred and that in the interim she had been deprived of all marketability and value without payment of just compensation. Finally, on December 31, 1976, ten days before the scheduled start of the inverse condemnation trial and over three years after the "communications," the State of California filed an eminent domain action against the Briggs property.

The filing of the condemnation actions, however, only marked the beginning of the extraordinary burdens of a landowner subjected to public acquisition. Over the next two years, over fifteen experts were retained by Briggs at a cost of over $250,000. These experts were retained to disprove charges by the State of California and its various agencies, officials, and employees, attacking the use, amenities, and value of her property. Suddenly the property, once listed as acquisition Priority 1-a in the State of California, was depreciated in the eyes of the jury by government consultants who suggested a value less than her purchase price a decade earlier.

The state government challenged every conceivable amenity of the property. The state questioned the feasibility of the use of the property as a hotel site (despite the fact the property was zoned for a hotel). The state cited the "detrimental impact of any development upon adjoining highway congestion (while at the same time the State of California encouraged the establishment of the federal park in neighboring Big Sur and the impact of nine million additional visitors on that same highway). The state questioned the availability of water (despite ample evidence of water available to the property). The state challenged the possible development of the property—despite the existence of an adjacent subdivision.

The trial court judge made a series of findings that were a grave and damning indictment of the conduct of the Coastal Commission.[54] The court heard uncontroverted evidence from local realtors, attorneys, and the owner herself that her property had been clouded, had become unmarketable, and had been denied all economic use. The court reviewed the evidence, and the testimony of numerous witnesses who delineated the history of this project. In the process, a subtle conspiracy came to light by which, in the name of the environment and park projects, a property had been rendered worthless.

In the spring of 1977 the trial judge ruled that the State of California was guilty of inverse condemnation, had destroyed the constitutional rights of Mrs. Mitzi S. Briggs, entitling her to an award of just compensation.[55] That trial judge found that the State of California, through its Department of Parks and Recreation and the Coastal Commission, had engaged in an attempt to preclude the use of her property in order to freeze it without payment of just compensation and without affording her the due process to which she was entitled under the United States Constitution. Moreover, the judge executed over fifty-five findings of fact and conclusions of law delineating the constitutional violations and the evidence, including countless documents and testimony that reflected a subtle conspiracy by government officials to destroy one citizens' constitutional rights.

After two years of extensive litigation and court costs, 5,000 hours of attorneys' time, and four phases of bifurcated trial hearings, a trial court awarded Mitzi S. Briggs $6.5 million of compensation. This unfortunately, did not resolve Mrs. Briggs' 4½ year battle. The trial result was appealed by the State of California and the acquisition process continued. In late 1979 a California appellate court reviewed the Briggs decision in light of the state's "environmental" justifications. Pitted against a state's goal of coastal preservation were the delineated abuses of government officials who had trampled the rights of another American.

The Court of Appeals found that "the judgment was based on an error of law" and reversed the Briggs judgment. The court confirmed the facts: (1) the denial of development and use by the Coastal Commission; (2) the secret telephone and telegram communications by the Department of Parks and Recreation; (3) the park director's assurances that the acquisition would follow after the passage of a bond act; and (4) the governor's authorization for funding. The court found a justification—a justification based on the intricacies of bureaucratic snags that would permit the government's delay in its acquisition of Briggs property. The court justified the state's delay upon various "difficulties" in completing studies, budget estimates and appraisals. Yet the court ignored the constitutional test: the impact on the individual's constitutional rights.

The appellate court ignored fifty-five findings of fact and conclusions of law delineating a virtual conspiracy to destroy constitutional rights. The court adopted a frightening policy while simultaneously discarding two hundred years of constitutional rights.

First, the court reasoned that since the Department of Parks was not technically sanctioned with the power of acquisition (an assignment reserved to an agency called the Public Works Board) then "as a matter of law, and at all times here pertinent, *no action by the Department alone could give rise to inverse condemnation liability.*" No action, nothing they could do, regardless of its effect, could give rise to the constitutional guarantee of just compensation.

Second, the court held that the compensation remedy was no longer appropriate. The court replaced the constitutional "compensation" remedy with one known as "writ of mandate." In a mandate action, the court would review the history of what took place and if found unconstitutional, direct the offending agency to hold another hearing. This theory, concocted by government attorneys and known as "the ping pong theory," would subject a landowner to years of litigation without relief. Thus, as the property remained without use, income, or marketability the owner would twirl in the courts in order to get a court determination that her constitutional rights had been destroyed. After having obtained that victory against an adamant agency, the landowner would return to that agency for a second hearing. Nothing would prevent the agency from repeating the wrong. The constitutional guarantee of compensation had been evaded in the name of the environment, as individual rights gave way to state goals.

The *AGINS* Case

The environmental onslaught against individual constitutional rights reached its pinnacle in *Agins* v. *the City of Tiburon.* In that case, the California Supreme Court, bolstered by a decade of erosion of constitutional rights, took the final step. Mr. and Mrs. Agins had sued the City of Tiburon, an affluent community along the northern part of San Francisco Bay, for inverse condemnation. They claimed that their ten-acre property had been downzoned by the city as a substitute for public acquisition and that the property had been rendered worthless as a result.

The California Supreme Court broke with two hundred years of constitutional guarantees and ruled as a matter of law, without evidence or testimony, that the Agins no longer could receive compensation. In effect, the court ruled that the remedy of invalidation had replaced the constitutional guarantee of compensation. The government and environmental lawyers had finally convinced the Supreme Court of one of our nation's most influencial states to abandon the constitution in the name of the environment. They imposed upon the Agins family a statutory remedy Writ of Mandate, "the ping pong theory," that they can engage in a three- to four-year battle to determine the constitutionality of the government's conduct, and if successful, return for another hearing. The owner must pursue administrative hearings, become its victim, prove the victimization in court, and then begin again.

What has happened to our system?

- How could American citizens be subjected to five to ten-minute hearings as conducted by the California Coastal Commission?

- How could a government impose virtual moratoriums upon the use and development of property without payment of compensation?

- How could a landowner be forced to dedicate land-holdings or money to government agencies in order to use his own property?

- How could a landowner be placed on a government acquisition list by an agency that had neither the funding nor legal authority to acquire property?

- How could the owners of Inglenook Fen be declared landowners of an Ice Age preserve and be banned from use of their property, only to find federal maps had been altered in an attempt to change a cattle watering hole into a sensitive environmental area?

- How could an "environmental" agency be allowed to establish hotel room rates and restaurant prices, or decree dedication of condominium units to the poor?

- How can the federal government continue to acquire private property holdings through decade-long acquisition programs during which the owner is blocked from use and development of his property without receiving any compensation?

- How can the federal government proceed with federal park projects which adversely affect the environment without any significant studies while a single homebuilder is put through years of time and expense for a solitary project?

- How can all land use be banned in the name of the environment without payment of just compensation?

How does one explain the erosion of individual constitutional rights by government conduct and its sponsors through judicial abdication? The ancient edict that "those who do not learn from history are doomed to relive it" has particular application. The erosion of property rights is a first step toward the demise of individual liberties.

When a legal system fails to maintain adequate safeguards for individual rights, the potential for injury is devastating. Whether it be the incarceration of Japanese Americans during World War II or the witch hunting fanaticism of McCarthyism in the 1950s, the results are intolerable. A free society depends upon the priority of individual rights over state or national goals. When government goals justify violation of individual rights, the system becomes a base for the excess of one's political philosophy. Can we ever be allowed to forget the lesson of Weimar Germany?

Pre-World War II Germany

The Weimar Republic of Germany guaranteed as a matter of constitutional law certain fundamental property rights as inviolate. Among those rights were the sanctity of individual home ownership and the concept that private property could not be expropriated by the government without payment of compensation.

On February 28, 1933, President von Hindenburg issued a presidential decree, in accordance with Adolf Hitler's demand. It suspended certain fundamental constitutional guarantees of the Weimar Republic, and the emergence of the Nazi state and degradation of constitutional rights had begun. The restrictions, which emanated from that presidential decree, were far-reaching restraints on liberty. They included orders for confiscation as well as restrictions on private property holdings.[56] Stricken from the constitution of the Weimar Republic were the following fundamental property rights:

> Article 115. Every German's home is his sanctuary and inviolable. Exceptions may only be made as provided by law.

> Article 153. Property is guaranteed by the Constitution. Its content and limits are defined by the law. Expropriation can only take place for the public benefit and on a legal basis. Adequate compensation shall be granted, unless a Reich law orders otherwise. In the case of a dispute concerning the amount of compensation, it shall be possible to submit the matter to the ordinary civil courts unless Reich laws determine otherwise.

> *Compensation must be paid if the Reich expropriates property* belonging to the lands, communes, or public utility associations. Property carried obligations. Its use shall also serve the common good.[57]

On September 15, 1935 a directive was issued entitled "Directions for Handling of the Jewish Question," which held that "the entire Jewish property is to be seized and confiscated with the exception of that which is necessary for a bare existence. As far as the economic situation permits, the power of disposal of their property is to be taken from the Jews as soon as possible through orders and other measures given by the Commissariat, so that the moving of property will quickly cease."[58]

Soon thereafter, not only were the constitutional rights curtailed, but the judicial system was impacted as well by the decrees and directives of the Nazi state. By 1936, members of the judiciary were being advised of the decisions and conduct expected of them as members under the control of the government.

On January 14, 1936 a directive of one Professor Karl Eckhardt, an editor of a legal journal, under the publishing name "Dr. Hans Frank" disclosed the following duty of the judiciary under the Third Reich:

1. The judge is not placed over the citizen as a representative of the State authority, but as a member of the living community of the German people. It is not his duty to help to enforce a law superior to the national community or to impose his system of universal values. His role is to safeguard the concrete order of the racial community, to eliminate dangerous elements, to prosecute all acts harmful to the community, and to arbitrate in disagreements between members of the community.

2. The National Socialist ideology, especially as expressed in the Party program and in the speeches of our Fuhrer, is the basis for interpreting legal sources.

3. *The judge has no right to scrutinize decisions made by the Fuhrer* and issued in the form of a law or decree. The judge is also bound by any other decisions of the Fuhrer which clearly express the intention of establishing law.[59] [Italics are the authors'.]

In addition, the extent to which German Nazi authority violated individual liberties and the right of compensation for the taking of property also created discrimination between those whose property holdings and liberties were curtailed as opposed to those who maintained individual liberties. Yet the Nazis undermined their existing legal system of the Weimar Republic and strenuously objected to principles such as equality before the law.[60] What occurred as a replacement to a system of individual rights, sanctity of private property holdings, and a ban against discrimination was a system of highly subjective, arbitrary, and confused rules dominated by political considerations and reviewed by a judiciary system "subservient to the regime'' which resulted "in the progressive undermining and perversion of law."[61]

The manner in which the German judicial system was degraded into an implementor of state goals and policies is of interest here, due to the erosion of civil and property rights in America "for the environment." Historians have concluded that the usurpation of judicial independence in Nazi Germany arose in part as a result of "the degradation of the judge into a mere agent of the state and to his transition to a 'civil servant' rather than a guardian of the rights of the individual and as someone who could be relied upon to interpret the law with a sense of justice."[62]

In addition, the judiciary and its role in German society were subverted by a series of national orders which restricted judges to agents of the state. On April 7, 1933 the Third Reich established the "law concerning the reconstruction of the professional civil service" which abolished "the principle that judges could not be dismissed or demoted for political reasons and thus undermine the principal of the independence of the judiciary.[63] Moreover, by virtue of the German civil service law of January 26, 1937, members of the judiciary were treated as civil servants who could be retired if they could not be relied upon to "support the national socialist state" of Germany.[64]

A countless number of commentators had sought to explain the incredible series of events by which a constitutional Weimar Republic was transferred into a state without private property or individual rights. An independent judiciary was subverted into an agent of the state and an instrument of the enforcement of state goals, regardless of their impact on individual and constitutional rights.

In a warning to the Western World, Professor Friedrich A. Hayek in *The Road to Serfdom* wrote in response to the end of Nazi Germany and the lesson learned of the impact on individual rights when government planners are allowed to tamper with the concept of private property:

> What our generation has forgotten is that the system of private property is the most important guarantee of freedom not only for those who own property, but scarcely less for those who do not. It is only because the control of the means of production is divided among many people acting independently that nobody has complete power over us, that we as individuals can decide what to do with ourselves. If all the means of production were vested in a single hand, whether it be nominally that of "society" as a whole or that of a dictator, whoever exercises this control has complete power over us.[65]

Moreover, Professor Hayek warned of the devastating impact of allowing centralized planning and idealists to govern, without restraint, the life of society. Although he recognized the value of planners, he forewarned the danger of planners, who as idealists, often become the most intolerant of the views of others and therefore are uncompromising individuals:

> From the saintly and single-minded idealist to the fanatic is often but a step . . . there could hardly be a more unbearable—and more irrational—world than one in which the most eminent specialists in each field were allowed to proceed unchecked with the realization of their ideals.[66]

It is a matter of international and moral law that no government official may rely upon orders that destroy individual and fundamental rights. Of particular concern from that historic lesson should be our realization that the American system is predicated upon a series of checks and balances. The judiciary must stand as a balance between the goals and desires and actions of government on the one hand and the individual constitutional guarantee of individuals on the other. The judiciary must *insure that no state goal, regardless of its validity or popular support, can usurp an individual fundamental freedom.*

At that point when the judiciary establishes state or national goals as a priority and reason for usurping individual rights, the constitutional guarantees, whether they be those of the Weimar Republic or those of the United States, become hollow promises. The society becomes an implementation of government without control or restraint. At best, we can only hope for a judiciary which enforces individual rights and in turn depends upon the decency of the individual members to assert a higher set of values regardless of prior judicial precedent or government-ordered policies.

What lesson was learned? We, like the citizens of the Weimar Republic, had a constitutional guarantee, a guarantee that a citizen's home was his sanctuary and that the government could not expropriate property without compensation. In the instance of Germany, the resulting deprivation of constitutional rights was not as swift as the Hitler-Hindenburg decrees would indicate. Despite the destruction of constitutional rights for private property holdings, the net effect was, as in our system, a gradual usurpation of constitutional rights. In Germany, "the legal system collapsed through a 'series' of *ad hoc* measures over years rather than by speedy and systematic reform," all of which "reflected the nature of the Nazi takeover of power with its quasi-legal emphasis on continuity. . . ."[67]

The erosion of constitutional rights in the United States appears to be happening rapidly, but in a random rather than a systematic program. The loss of rights has not been demonstrated by any one decision or any one event. It has occurred in planning commission and city council hearings, in court rooms and by agency staffs across our nation. These rights have been replaced by the demands and goals of government. The changes that have occurred in constitutional rights of private property holdings have been subtle, without mass notoriety, or notice.

In the Nuremburg trials that followed World War II the United States imposed an international decree without historic precedent. We affirmed the priority of fundamental human rights and dignity above state goals. We confirmed an understanding that no governmental official could rely upon state goals or national goals to the exclusion of individual fundamental rights. The principle applied with greatest significance to a judicial system. Our system was predicated on the belief that the judiciary stood as a buffer between the unfair goals and plans of government and the sanctity of individual rights. The value, however noble, of one could not justify the destruction or usurpation of the other.

Summary

Historically we have recognized the fundamental nature of private property and its link to earned liberty. We have imposed in part the doctrine of laissez faire, the sanctity of property of John Locke, a confirmation of Alistair Cooke's view that when everything was said and done, America was not a creation of freedom of speech and religion alone, but a struggle of individualists to achieve their own possessions through personal sacrifice and labor. We confirmed that property rights were as fundamental as any other right and when the property earned through the labor of one's life was confiscated, then the value of that life was also confiscated.

If we can, in the name of the environment and in the name of public ownership of private lands, in the name of parks, open space, and nature, usurp, destroy, or alter individual rights without remedy, then the same can occur in the name of some other state or national goals. In the final analysis we must ask if the eradication of individual rights of a minority people in Germany is any different in concept than the destruction of individual property rights in the name of the new religion "the environment." Has the American private property owner become the Japanese Americans of WW II, the victims of McCarthyism, or the German Jew of the 1930s? Of even greater concern: is the last great buffer and protector of individual rights, our court system, becoming an instrument of government policy?

Chapter Seven

Is It Working?

The environmental movement had a worthy goal of attempting to prevent misuse of our resources and the environment. However, the successes that have been achieved do not justify the abuse of power and civil rights, the over-regulation, and wasteful bureaucracy, the cost to consumers, and the vast expenditures of taxpayers' money that have transpired.

Environmental Health Standards

Environmental groups and agencies often set higher environmental quality standards than are actually necessary to protect the public's health. Administrative agencies frequently overlook the economic hardship these standards cause the public. Air quality standards and regulations are often used as tools to stop projects and urban growth unnecessarily. A good example of this is found in the legal fight over the California Air Resources Board's air quality standards, often used as an instrument to frustrate growth.

The *Wall Street Journal* reported on November 18, 1980 a decision by Judge Eugene Sax in Los Angeles on two of California's strict air quality standards. The judge ruled that the California Air Resources Board must rescind its stringent standards regarding sulphur dioxide and sulphate. Sax based his ruling on findings that the California sulphur dioxide standards were three times as stringent as the federal standards and were not justified by evidence showing they were needed to protect the public health. The judge also found that hearings on the ARB's standards violated proper procedures because the public wasn't given adequate notice of the planned actions nor enough time to evaluate staff reports supporting the actions. The judge further ruled that the ARB must consider the economic implications of its standards before adopting them.

Sax ruled that although Governor Jerry Brown's administration and the ARB had the right to set stiffer air quality standards for California than had been set for the rest of the United States, it had to prove the need for these standards.

In the case of oil companies such as Mobil, C & L Corporation, Gulf Oil Corporation, and Standard Oil Company of California, in conjunction with independent oil producing groups, it was contended that these "two air quality standards [of the California Air Resources Board] would cause them [the oil companies] to spend billions of dollars on pollution control equipment, but wouldn't improve public health."

Air quality and other environmental standards are obviously needed to maintain an environment that is healthy. But we do not need standards set arbitrarily that provide little benefit to the public. Agency administrators must act in a reasonable and responsible manner and not take advantage of their position for their "cause."

The Environmental Protection Hustle

Professor Bernard Frieden of M.I.T., in his book *The Environmental Protection Hustle,*[68] stated that in the San Francisco Bay Area between 1972–75, environmental lawsuits held up construction of over 20,000 dwelling units. The net effect, he said, was not to improve the environment but to harm it. He found that environmental regulations encouraging low-density, single-family housing drove housing costs up without improving the environment by using more land for fewer homes. He also found that the regulations drove up the cost of land because less land was available for the construction of houses.

Frieden noted that environmentalists were very possessive of other people's property and felt great moral righteousness. They were not concerned with fairness or other people's interests or rights. Dr. Frieden found that although environmental groups stated they were not against growth, in reality they were against growth and wanted to stop development.

Environmental groups have worked to achieve their goals by some of the following methods:

1. Pushing for 20-, 40- and even 60-acre lot sizes;
2. Demanding utility moratoriums that created severe problems for public agencies and private landholders;
3. Restricting the service boundaries, therefore controlling population;
4. Pushing for high development fees (in some areas, fees ran as high as $15,000 per house);
5. Working for growth quotas;
6. Extending the environmental review process, which gave opportunities to opponents to slow down or stop projects (some projects took as long as nine years to be processed through the environmental review process);
7. Initiating lawsuits at any stage of the review process of a project.

In his book Dr. Frieden notes that environmentalists are not concerned that their actions forced housing to cost more. Generally, environmentalists themselves were economically comfortable and lived in expensive homes.

Less growth only increased the value of their property. Frieden found that environmentalists advocate sacrifice for others, but not themselves. He feels that the environmentalist movement has been carried to extremes at the expense of the public and was out of balance with public need.

Dr. Frieden found in his studies[69] (as did Metzger) that claims by environmental groups that there was an *endangered species* on a project site, often proved false upon investigation. In numerous cases, there was an "endangered red herring" set up to delay a project. Environmental groups frequently state that a project area *might* be the habitat for an endangered species, even though none had ever been seen on the site.

Antiproject oriented Environmental Impact Reports (EIRs) frequently eliminate any mention of *benefits* of a project. An impact statement should consider the *total* environment, including social and economic environmental analysis. In one project on land having no existing trees, the EIR writer refused to mention that thousands of trees and shrubs would be planted by the developer and that the new trees would provide additional food and nesting habitat for birds. The same EIR writer made a big issue over the natural grasses on the site—in this case foxtail weeds—saying that they would be harmed and that the rodents and ground squirrels would be displaced by the housing development. When challenged with the fact that thousands of trees and shrubs would be planted, increasing the habitat for birds, he replied that the type of birds attracted to the shrubs and trees were *of no importance.*

Moss Landing

At Moss Landing in California, a combination of government bureaucracies (the California Coastal Commission and federal land authorities) consistently deferred and precluded plans for extensive development and rehabilitation of the coastal wetlands into commercial recreational water-oriented facilities out of fear that an endangered three-toed salamander habitat would be harmed. That the salamander had *never been seen,* nor his existence been verified, did not matter. The "salamander herring" was a tool to curtail development of the Moss Landing area.

Costs and Benefits of Environmental Controls

Even with its power and expenditures the actual benefits of efforts to save the environment are questionable. Studies of water and air improvement are especially disturbing. Studies commissioned by President Carter's Council on Environmental Quality found it difficult to identify clearly the benefits of air and water pollution control efforts. The Commission for Environment Quality's report in 1979,[70] indicated that, after expressing estimates in the 1978 dollar value and standardizing for a 20 percent improvement in air quality, the estimates of the health benefits of controlling air pollution from stationary sources ranged from $1.8 billion to $14.4 billion. C.E.Q. hired a consultant to conduct a benefit study in 1979. Assuming a high health benefit, the study estimated the annual benefits in 1978 from measured improvements in air quality since 1970 could be reasonably valued at $21.4 billion. Of this total, $17 billion represented reductions in mortality and morbidity, $2 billion reduced soiling and cleaning costs, $700,000 increased agricultural output, $900,000 prevention of corrosion and other material damage, and $800,000 increases in property values.

Because of the method of implementing water control programs, the CEQ report estimated the *total annual benefits* to be realized by 1985 as a result of the country's water pollution control legislation at about *$12.3* billion per year, with recreational benefits amounting to about $6.7 billion per year of the total. CEQ estimated that between

1970 and 1979, "federal environmental legislation added on the average slightly more than three-tenths of one percentage point to the annual rate of increase of the CIP (Consumer Price Index)." The study estimated that between 1979 and 1986, federal environmental regulations would add between one and two-tenths of one percentage point to the annual inflation rate.

The CEQ report indicated also that after 1977 the costs of air and water pollution control expenditures "began to exert some drag on the economy," and by 1986 real GNP in the "with controls" scenario is predicted to reduce the GNP $24.5 billion per year, or one percent lower than in the "without controls" scenario. In other words, pollution controls will have a negative impact on the economy that will increase from 1978 to 1986. There was no attempt to measure the years after 1986.

CEQ's Tenth Annual Report stated that the nation's air quality was improving but their data was not reassuring. The data CEQ used came from EPA's "The Cost of Clean Air and Water." The combined data from twenty-five major metropolitan areas indicated that the number of "unhealthful" days declined by only 15 percent between 1974 and 1977, while the number of "very unhealthful" days declined 32 percent. Data from approximately fifty of the most polluted counties across the country, however, showed that violations of ambient air quality standards generally either remained the same or decreased between 1974 and 1977.

In a study made in 1977, CEQ reports that the air in two of the forty-one urban areas for which reliable data were available (New York and Los Angeles) still registered in the unhealthful range for more than two out of every three days of the year. In three urban areas, air pollution appeared to have grown worse between 1974 and 1977. Unfortunately, Los Angeles had some of its worst days of air pollution in September and October of 1980.

In an analysis of the U.S. Geological Survey data, CEQ finds that the water quality in the United States is merely staying the same since the early 1970s. The study reports that "there has been little or no overall change in the levels of five major water pollution indicators over the four years between 1975 and 1978."[71]

To determine the progress of water pollution controls, CEQ made an examination of the trends in water pollution at forty-four selected cities on major rivers. Of 149 comparisons they made of violation rates, sixty-nine showed improvement in water quality, forty-one showed degradation, and thirty-nine showed no change.

CEQ indicated further that as many as two-thirds of the nation's lakes may have serious pollution problems. An estimated 80 percent of more than 3,700 urban lakes in the United States are significantly degraded.[72]

Based on the findings and data in the Council on Environmental Quality's Tenth Annual Report, there appears to have been some improvement in our environment. But apparently the nation has a long way to go, however, before significant improvement can be made in air and water quality in the problem areas of the United States. Simply put, our nation is spending huge sums to improve the environment but apparently isn't making much progress.

At the same time money is spent to create programs to "save the environment," the cost of complying with all existing federal pollution control and environmental quality programs in 1978 is estimated to be $26.9 billion. The Council on Environmental Quality further estimates that over a ten-year period from 1978 to 1989, total incremental spending in response to all federal environmental programs is projected to be $477.6 billion. In 1987, the total annual costs of estimated incremental pollution abatement alone would be $64 billion (See Figure 23.)[73]

In the same report, CEQ estimated that the total pollution abatement and environmental quality expenditures for 1978 through 1987 would amount to *$710.7 billion.* The total estimated annual costs by 1987 would be $94.2 billion. The costs of environmental controls are clearly higher than the benefits received by CEQ estimates.

In the 1979 report (page 665), CEQ further comments that: "Regardless of their initial impacts, the cost of pollution control is born by the citizens of the United States. There are no disembodied entities called 'industry' or 'environment' that really bear the costs. The final burden comes to rest on individuals."

Could the federal government, with revised and more reasonable environmental goals and priorities, obtain more identifiable environmental protection and improvements with less money?

Environmental Regulation Impact

In an article in *Saturday Review* Robert Crandall, Senior Fellow at the Brookings Institution,[74] indicated that in ten years Congress had created a "federal bureaucracy employing 80,000 people, with the mission of protecting the environment and consumers or workers from harm."

Figure 23: Estimated incremental pollution abatement and environmental quality expenditures, 1978–1987[1] (in billions of 1978 dollars).

	1978			1987			Cumulative (1978–87)			
	Operation and Maintenance	Annual Capital Costs[2]	Total Annual Costs	Operation and Maintenance	Annual Capital Costs[2]	Total Annual Costs	Capital Investment	Operation and Maintenance	Capital Costs[2]	Total Costs
Air Pollution										
Public	0.9	0.3	1.2	2.0	0.8	2.8	4.6	13.7	5.5	19.2
Private										
Mobile	4.3	3.3	7.6	5.1	9.3	14.4	59.6	45.0	66.4	111.4
Industrial	2.3	2.7	5.0	3.7	5.2	8.9	28.6	44.1	38.6	82.7
Utilities	1.6	1.2	2.8	6.5	4.8	11.3	26.4	37.5	28.1	65.6
Subtotal	9.1	7.5	16.6	17.3	20.1	37.4	119.2	140.3	138.6	278.9
Water Pollution										
Public	1.5	3.0	4.5	2.1	5.0	7.1	17.2	16.6	46.7	63.3
Private										
Industrial	2.1	1.6	3.7	5.7	4.6	10.3	28.0	38.9	30.4	69.3
Utilities	1.2	0.8	2.0	1.8	1.2	3.0	3.9	16.0	10.1	26.1
Subtotal	4.8	5.4	10.2	9.6	10.8	20.4	68.5	71.5	87.2	158.7
Solid Waste										
Public	NA	NA	NA	0.5	0.3	0.8	NA	3.5	2.2	5.7
Private	NA	NA	NA	1.2	0.6	1.8	NA	8.8	4.7	13.5
Subtotal	NA	NA	NA	1.7	0.9	2.6	NA	12.3	6.9	19.2
Toxic Substances	0.1	NA	0.1	0.3	NA	0.3	NA	2.2	NA	2.2
Drinking Water	<.05	<.05	<.05	0.4	0.4	0.8	NA	2.9	2.7	5.6
Noise	<.05	<.05	<.05	0.6	1.0	1.6	4.8	2.5	4.1	6.6
Pesticides	<.05	<.05	<.05	0.1	<.05	0.1	NA	0.4	<.05	0.4
Land Reclamation	NA	NA	NA	0.8	NA	0.8	NA	6.0	NA	6.0
Total	14.0	12.9	26.9	30.8	33.2	64.0	192.5	238.1	239.5	477.6

NA = Not Available

[1] Incremental costs are those made in response to federal environmental legislation beyond those that would have been made in the absence of that legislation.

[2] Interest and depreciation.

* Sources: Environmental Quality, 10th Annual Report of Council on Environmental Quality.

He found that federal agencies were not interested in calculating the costs of their regulations. He estimated the cost of complying with EPA regulations in 1976 totaled about $15 billion and in 1980 would cost $40 billion per year.

Another member of the prestigious Brookings Institution, Edward Denison, estimated that "productivity growth was reduced by nearly 20 percent in 1975 owing to increasing environmental control costs and health safety regulations imposed upon private non-farm business.[75] Denison estimated business spent about $9 billion alone on environmental control in 1975 but would spend four to five times that amount per year by the mid-1980s if EPA fully enforces the laws.

Consumer advocate Ralph Nader acknowledged that environmental regulations have generated costs to the public when he stated: "In fact, regulation provides the largest source of new jobs in industry today. Regulation has created perhaps a million jobs and eliminated no more than 15,000 to 20,000.[76]

Mr. Nader fails to mention that these are *non-productive* jobs that add costs to the products purchased by consumers. The consumer indirectly pays for their salaries.

Crandall emphasizes this point: "We have considerable evidence that growing social regulation could eat into our ability to grow economically. Productivity growth has slowed to about 1 percent per year, a rate which permits very little improvement in the average standard of living and even less ability to address other pressing social problems. There can be little doubt that regulation has contributed to this sharp deceleration in growth."[77]

Crandall found that agency environmentalists cleverly hid the costs of regulation from the public by the manner in which they wrote regulations. The agencies deliberately mandated standards for business, knowing that the cost of compliance would be added to the product's price. If a pollution tax or insurance scheme had been used, he felt that, to comply, firms could have been forced to devise environmental and health standards and the costs of programs.

Cost of Federal Requirements

The Advisory Committee on Intergovernment Relations also found that the cost of environmental controls was high. Figure 24 shows the estimated cost of federal regulation for environment and pollution abatement to consumers, government, and business.

The Commission on Federal Paperwork did a study on the

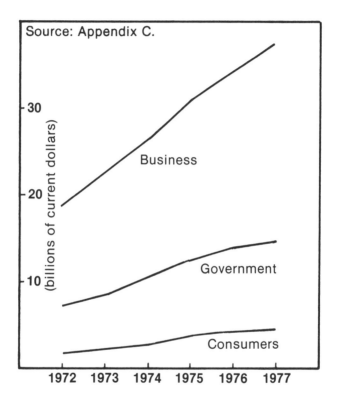

Source: Appendix C.

Business

Government

Consumers

(billions of current dollars)

30

20

10

1972 1973 1974 1975 1976 1977

Figure 24: Costs of federal regulation—pollution abatement
and control. (Private and public spending for
pollution abatement and control.)

regulation costs of federal paperwork burden on individuals, businesses, and state and local government and found it to be substantial. The commission estimated the costs at more than $100 billion a year in 1977 and estimated that $10 billion of the burden was unnecessary.[78] The commission found that regulatory paperwork cost could be broken down as follows:

Federal government:	$43 billion/yr.
Private industry:	$25–$32 billion/yr.
State and local government:	$5–$9 billion/yr.
Individuals:	$8.7 billion/yr.
Farmers:	$350 million/yr.
Labor organizations:	$75 million/yr.

Figure 25: Federal regulatory paperwork costs in 1977.

Costs and Benefits of Environmental Regulations Locally

On the local scene, federal, state, and local government regulations and programs have increased building costs substantially, as a result of delays, environmental reviews, fees and permits, additional design and offsite amenities, and open space requirements.

A study by the Construction Industry Research Board, located in Los Angeles, concerning growth restrictions and new home prices,[79] found that the impact on the price of homes due to restriction of growth amounted to 18 percent of the cost of a home in 1979, or an increase from $82,700 to $94,100. The study indicated that in 1982 the cost of a home due to restricted growth practices by communities would increase the price of a home by 27 percent or from $98,500 to $125,000.

In a study entitled "Growth Management"[80] conducted by Dr. Richard Ellison for the Urban Land Institute in 1979, an analysis was made of the impact of San Diego's Growth Management Plan on housing costs in that area. Dr. Ellison, Assistant Director for Urban Economics in the "Sensible Growth Department" of the National Association of Homebuilders, described two growth patterns under the San Diego plan, one was called "Restrictive Growth Management" and the second, which was more severe, was called "Slow Growth Policy."

The study considered not only the historical housing growth pattern in the San Diego area from 1970–77, it analyzed the impact from 1978 to 1979 and identified the effect on lots, housing costs, and employment. Dr. Ellison found there was an increase in finished lot prices to the consumer of 3.5 percent under the restrictive growth program and 10 percent greater with the slow growth policy. See Figure 26, "Average Price of Finished Lots (Single-Family)."

When considering a single-family home, Ellison's study found that there was about a 5 percent increase in the price of a new home, or an amount of $5,300 per home. This amounted to a total of about 8.5 percent to 15 percent maximum. The results of the model study "demonstrated that managed-growth policies that restrict the supply of housing will add significantly to housing costs." See Figure 27, "Average Price of Single-Family Homes."

Dr. Ellison's study also measured the employment levels and lost man-years over a two-year period. The study showed that when housing starts were reduced to 20,000 units per year (restrictive growth policy), 4,725 jobs would be lost. Under the slow growth policy (11,300 units), the figure increased to 23,000 lost jobs. Losses in income during the two-year period equalled approximately $110 million and $705 million under the two restrictive growth policies. See Figure 28, "Total Employment (not seasonally adjusted)."

Dr. Ellison found that growth limitation would not provide any benefits to the City of San Diego: "It is clear that reductions in population and housing starts would not confer significant physical advantage to local governments. On the contrary, a policy of moderate growth appears to be the most reasonable course of action."

The Urban Land Institute study found that a comprehensive growth management policy can be beneficial if the following conditions are met: (1) an adequate capital improvement and expansion program is planned and implemented to accommodate, not limit, anticipated growth; (2) incentives are formed to draw capital, people, and housing to infill; and core areas are used, rather than disincentives levied against suburban development; (3) a sufficient supply of developable land is designated to meet housing and reserve needs, thus moderating speculative and monopolistic influences on land prices; and (4) it is recognized that infilling and redevelopment will provide only marginal increases in housing stock and will not likely appeal to the largest segment of the market.

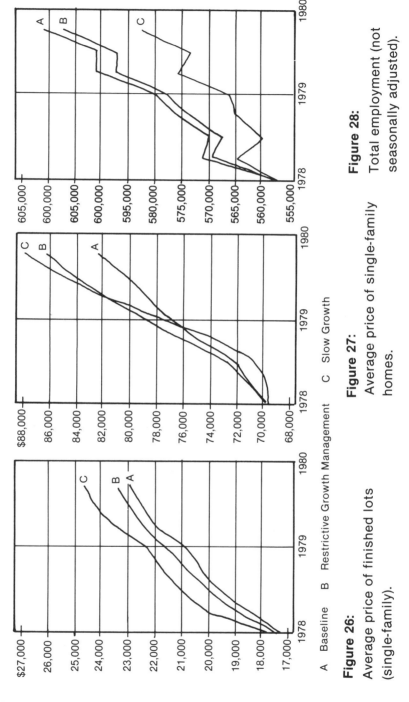

A   Baseline   B   Restrictive Growth Management   C   Slow Growth

Figure 26:
Average price of finished lots (single-family).

Figure 27:
Average price of single-family homes.

Figure 28:
Total employment (not seasonally adjusted).

Environmental Impact Reports—Cost to Consumers

Unfortunately, the Environmental Impact Report (EIR) process has become a tool for the stop-growth forces and preservationists, an abuse by which the EIR permits groups to challenge, with little personal expense, large and costly projects. The EIR process has made officials, developers, and the public more aware of environmental issues and prevented poorly conceived projects, but at a steep price. Irresponsible public officials, with assistance from environmentalists, using the EIR process for their environmental goals, have delayed and stopped projects, driving up the costs of housing for consumers, commercial, and industrial projects. Figure 29 illustrates the time involved in processing a typical EIR study.

The New York Land Institute in New York State found that an Environmental Impact Statement for an average fifty-unit subdivision costs about $50,000 and takes six months to a year to be processed. The EIR for the expansion plan of the Los Angeles International Airport cost over $800,000 and took more than four years to complete.

The principal elements of EIR costs are document preparation, review and administration, delay costs, costs of uncertainty, and mitigation costs. In a study of the California Environmental Quality Act and the Cost of Delay for the Construction Industry Research Board by Environmental Analysis Systems, it was found that the EIR process in California in 1974 cost the *consumer* between $115 and $140 million.

The *Government Regulations and Housing Costs*[81] study conducted by the Rutgers University Center for Urban Policy Research in 1977, found that "19.7 percent of the purchase price of a house may be related to government regulatory excesses of one form or another." The Rutgers study, concerned with single-family houses priced at $50,000, found excess costs totaled $9,844. A purchase of a $100,000 home would be paying about $19,700 for *unnecessary* government regulations.

Costs to Government

There are naturally costs to government for the staffs to prepare EIRs and to administer the paperwork and public hearings. But government costs are passed on to taxpayers in higher taxes and fees. Increased government costs—federal, state, and local—are of course one of the reasons for our high inflation rate.

149

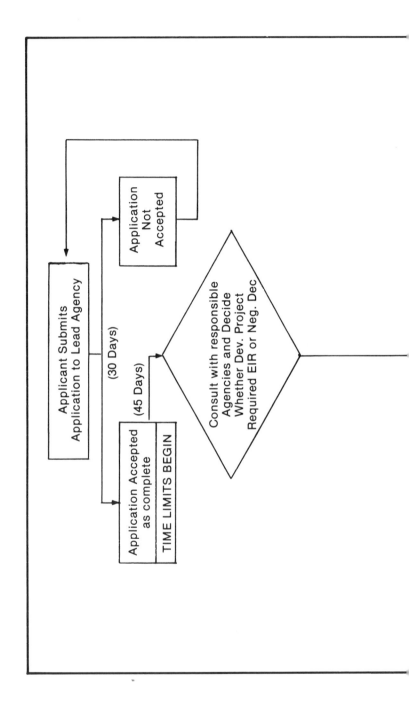

Figure 29: Guidelines for processing permits for development projects.

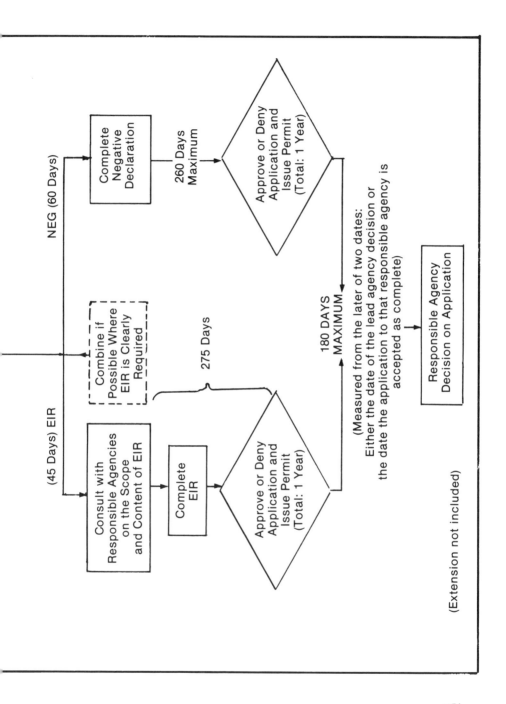

The Maze of Regulations

The specific purpose type of regulations of various government agencies demand new permits and fees which mean delays and higher costs to the consumer and taxpayer. A study by Dan K. Richardson,[82] *The Cost of Environmental Protection,* at the Center for Urban Policy Research, Rutgers University, found that in New Jersey it took thirty-eight permits to build a single-family home. The increase in average processing time for a residential project in New Jersey changed from 5 months in 1970 to 13.3 months in 1975.[83] The New Jersey experience is similar to government operations in most other parts of the country.

To "save the environment" the consumer is paying a high price. It is not clear that the quality of living for most people is improving in relationship to that cost. The taxpayers, not fully knowing the real costs or how to combat them, continue to support a costly, bureaucratic maze.

The Impact of EIRs on World Landmarks

If the nation's environmental policies and guidelines, especially those of the California Coastal Commission, were applied internationally, major landmarks would be eliminated or changed drastically. In the great port cities of San Francisco, London, and Hong Kong there would be great loss of charm. In San Francisco there would be no Golden Gate Bridge and no Fisherman's Wharf. In London there would be no Houses of Parliament or Scotland Yard buildings adjacent to the Thames. In Paris there would be no Eiffel Tower or Notre Dame Cathedral. The great resort areas of Monaco and Cannes would be devastated. There would be no grand homes along the ocean in Newport, Rhode Island or along the Hudson River. In New York there would be no Empire State Building and no United Nations Building. There would be no Naval Academy in Annapolis or Military Academy in West Point.

There would be no Swiss or Austrian hillside villages. The great Greek Island communities of Mykonos and Pathos would lose their waterfront charm. The Greeks in Athens would have to do without the Parthenon. In Istanbul the St. Sophia and the Blue Mosques would have to go. The nations of the world are lucky that the environmental movement did not predate the great architectural structures.

Many creative projects have been denied construction or destroyed by unimaginative, bureaucratic, stop-growth attitudes of officials and preservationists. Officials need to seek a balanced approach and use reason in analyzing projects. This can be done by encouraging sensitively designed facilities that also consider valid environmental needs.

The environment is an integrated part of our lives, but only *part* of our lives. The economic concerns of our communities, business, and industrial productivity, as well as our housing and labor needs, must be considered equally with "environmental needs." Irresponsible environmental organizations, unthinking legislators, and agency officials have generated too many unnecessary regulations and an environmentally-oriented bureaucracy that has cost the taxpayers and consumers a huge sum. It will take a generation to amortize the costs.

Chapter Eight

The Backlash

The environmental movement, the efforts to save the air, water, land, and coastal resources were necessary reactions to problems without boundaries. But the cost of the remedy may have exceeded the illness. The no-growth philosophy which prevailed in the 1970s had a negative impact on the cost of land and housing, caused a dramatic growth in government employees, regulations and appropriations, and eroded individual constitutional rights.

The 1970s witnessed the entrenchment of the environmental movement in regulatory codifications and dominance of federal and state bureaucracies throughout the nation. Those who opposed the excesses of government and the erosion of individual constitutional and civil rights were often considered "enemies of the people" and against conservation and ecology.

However, the extremism of certain environmental groups and the now-apparent cost to the consumer, landowner, and local government provide an incentive to a more accurate analysis of the environmental movement. For the first time, the motivations, conduct, and programs of environmentalists are being subjected to the same scrutiny as that faced by private enterprise.

Much of the skyrocketing cost of housing and rental accommodations and the lack of affordable housing units is attributable to federal and state acquisition of private properties and excessive and expensive land and housing regulations of local governments. One need not possess a master's degree in economics to understand the concept of supply and demand and thus appreciate the relationship of government restriction of supply to the cost to those in demand. Qualified appraisers will tell you that California state coastal policies have greatly increased the value of beach properties that are developable and reduced property values drastically where development has been stopped.

Is it any wonder that housing units in our most scenic areas are becoming refuges for the affluent? When the federalization of Alaska is completed, only a few will be able to afford the extensive exploratory vacation through uncharted wilderness: the rich, the affluent. When the remaining coastal resources of California are transferred into public domain, who will afford the few remaining homes and landholdings? Certainly not the middle class or laborers of our society. How will the poor and middle class visit these vast park holdings if energy costs preclude travel and regulations preclude commercial hotel and motel establishments? Is it any wonder then that the major environmental groups are dominated by professionals, doctors, lawyers, and accountants, rather than blacks, Hispanics, poor, young, and the middle class. Have we been subjected to "the environmental protection hustle" in the words of Professor Bernard Frieden in which large landholdings have been reserved as enclaves for the rich?

In the name of the environment, we were told to restrict densities of developments, encourage open space, preclude use, down-zone for a cleaner and more healthy environment. But whose environment? The environment of rich homeowners and landowners who had already secured their development and no longer wanted to share their pleasant environment? The most ardent environmental zeal lies in plush California communities such as Marin, San Mateo, and Malibu where homes average over $300,000 and all remaining land is precluded from development in the name of the environment. Is it any wonder then that the same communities that boast the strongest environmental concerns share the highest inflationary housing rate?

That same environmental zeal has impacted our business productivity. The environmental controls and over-regulation that developed in the 1970s created higher prices for products and helped fuel our present inflationary cycle and cost of living. In general, the cost of running a business has been greatly increased during the 1970s due to consumer and environmental advocates.

On October 28, 1980 an article in the *Wall Street Journal* accented the decline of America's productivity growth as exemplified by one company: Goodyear Tire and Rubber Company. In one week, the company's computer center "cranked out 345,000 pages of jargon-filled paper weighing 3,200 pounds—all to meet one new regulation of the Occupational Safety and Health Administration. The regulation required that employees have access to data on exposure to chemicals used in their plants.''

The Goodyear Company calculated that ''complying with regulations of six of the more demanding federal agencies cost $35.5 million in 1979, and that just filling out the required reports chewed up thirty-four employee years.''

The *Journal* reported that a study made by ''The Business Roundtable,'' a corporate executive group, showed that compliance costs for forty-eight major companies for 1977 were $2.6 billion *over and above* what good corporate citizens normally would have spent for environmental protection, employee health and safety, and other matters if the six government agencies hadn't intervened.'' The *Journal* quoted some economists who projected ''that the extra cost for all business exceeded $100 billion.''

The *Journal* found that many companies felt tighter environmental regulations, made even more difficult by constantly changing rules, ''were another government damper on productivity in the 1970s. New plants frequently were delayed six months to a year, and some far longer, as companies sought construction permits. Thousands of employee hours were devoured just getting all the permits, and the 'old, less efficient' plants operated that much longer. A few executives confide that they were dissuaded from building at all rather than face the hassle and personal vilification sometimes encountered when companies sought permits to build foundries, chemical plants, and other facilities with a reputation for pollution.''

The concept of local government autonomy and efficiency has been ruptured by virtue of excessive, overlapping, and at times incomprehensible federal environmental regulations. The increase of federal agencies and mandates (see Figures 9 and 10, ''Growth in Federal Regulations'') imposed a vast array of red tape upon local governments. This growth has been accompanied by extensive federal aid (see Figures 11 and 12, ''Growth in Federal Aid'') often conditioned without regard to the fact that the sources of the federal aid were the same community taxpayers suddenly regulated in the use of their own money.

The environmental movement has achieved a degree of hypocrisy in its irreverent opposition to energy production in all its forms. While our nation stands perilously close to Armageddon over limited production and unlimited costs of Middle East oil, our ardent environmentalists use every conceivable political, media, legislative, and judicial lever to oppose exploration of our own untapped mineral resources. Nuclear power plants are opposed for fear of Three Mile Island-type accidents and the problem of waste disposal. Oil exploration is opposed lest an occasional oil spill threaten a beach or oil pipeline interfere with the migration of Alaskan caribou, while an abundance of coal is buried from productivity for fear of air pollution. A nation built upon multiple use of natural and mineral resources now hoists its own economic impalement on the petard of environmental niceties, while our youth register for what could be the ultimate confrontation in the Middle East.

The greatest concern must rest with the impact upon individuals and their rights by the *excesses* of the environmental movement. Ours is a society of individuals, and when a national or state goal usurps their rights, our concept of a constitutional government is on its way to termination.

What Happened to the Victims of the Movement

Mitzi S. Briggs

The tragedy of Mrs. Briggs came to completion in December 1980, over 7 1/2 years after the first interference with her property rights by the California Coastal Commission. After facing a new lengthy trial and on the verge of bankruptcy, Mrs. Briggs was forced to come to an agreement with the state. The Public Works Board of the State of California approved a settlement in the sum of approximately $3.8 million for the purchase of her Carmel property in Monterey County, property worth $8 to $10 million in 1980 if allowed to be developed. As a result of that settlement, the State of California finally acquired the 36-acre ocean frontage in order to maintain it in a raw, open condition without any private use. The State of California incurred over $1 million in court costs, attorneys' times, and legal battles attributable to the earlier conduct of the Coastal Commission. The county and state would forever be deprived of tax revenue from a legally constituted commercial use of the property. The public would be deprived of a magnificent resort hotel with public amenities, parking lots, tennis courts, and public vistas and walks to encourage maximum use of the coast for all income groups. The public lost. But, just as importantly, an individual, Mitzi S. Briggs, suffered personally the destruction of her family assets, the violation of her constitutional rights, and fear and uncertainty for 7 1/2 years at the hands of a wealthy, powerful and determined state agency. Is this the justice our forefathers envisioned for Americans in 1776?

Cannery Row

On November 26, 1980, four cannery buildings were destroyed by fire as the owner, Dale Runyan, sustained $1.5 million in damages. The fire had been forewarned by City of Monterey officials years earlier, but the rehabilitation of the buildings was thwarted by the senseless antics of the Coastal Commission.

Cannery Row remains in rubble and deterioration as a true landmark to a seven-year effort of environmentalists to "save the coast."

Santa Monica Mountains National Recreation Area

In early 1981 the Reagan Administration announced the cessation of further federal funds for expansion of the SMMRA. By June of 1981 news reports circulated that the National Park Service, which had initially suggested to Congress $150 million for acquisition costs of the 150,000 acres, had always had its own private estimates of an acquisition cost in excess of $660 million. The inspector general of the Department of Interior has sealed the park files as a formal investigation proceeds.

Stearns Wharf

Stearns Wharf is now being completed as a mini-commercial establishment run by government officials rather than by private enterprise at a minimum loss of $75,000 a year to the public. Private enterprise was deprived of a public-commercial use after six years of attempts to seek approval. A private investment capable of generating a successful commercial venture attractive to the public was replaced by a government boondoggle.

Big Sur, California

It would appear that Big Sur legislation for a federal park has been stopped or at least thwarted in great part by the opposition led by Senator S. I. Hayakawa of California against the Burton-Cranston park machine. The overwhelming opposition of 98 percent of the landowners to the legislation had crescendoed into a temporary realization that the legislation sought was needless. The legislation and its future now await the control of President Reagan and the vow of Senator Cranston to return and try again.

Sagebrush Rebellion

On November 20–22, 1980, a conference was held in Salt Lake City by an organization known as LASER (League for the Advancement of States' Equal Rights). The first steps were taken by LASER towards an organized effort to divest the control and maintenance of lands in the federal public domain (excluding parks and wildernesses) to the control of the western states. The meeting, led by United States senators and endorsed by the President-elect Reagan, a self-proclaimed rebel, was attended by leading experts throughout the United States in the field of law, mining, ranching, economics, and education who sought a solution to unreasonable regulation.

Federal Park Acquisitions

In July 1981 Senator Malcolm Wallop conducted senate workshop hearings concerning the abuses of federal park officials and the extent of federal land acquisitions.

The Law

The judicial precedents established by the environmental movement pose the most serious challenge to our Constitution since the country's founding. Our judicial system has sanctioned a series of procedures, regulations, and government conduct in the name of a national goal. In this process, our courts have established a frightening precedent for the destruction of individual rights in the name of state-sponsored public goals.

If citizens can be subjected to five- or ten-minute hearings, extortion, voting irregularities, fraud, and virtual confiscation of their property in the name of preserving the public's environment, then why not in the name of religion, ethnic superiority, military preparedness, or some other "movement"? Even in the darkest days of the depression or the world wars, except for the unfair internment of Japanese-Americans, citizens were not treated with the same callous disregard of constitutional rights as has been justified in the name of preserving salamanders, garter snakes, and the migration habits of the Alaskan caribou.

Are the indignities perpetrated on Briggs, on Lynch, the Inholders, and Alaskans any different in the final analysis than the incarceration of Japanese-Americans in World War II, or racial discrimination in public facilities, or our treatment of the American Indians? The landowners who became victims of the faulty justice system probably feel as Chief Sitting Bull did when he said: "They made us many promises, more than I can remember, but they never kept but one; they promised to take our land, and they took it."

A New Direction

The activities of the environmental extremists in powerful government positions and the cries of the victims soon generated a large and growing group of citizens hurt directly, or at least angered, by unfair tactics. A backlash manifested itself suddenly with the election of Ronald Reagan to the Presidency and a Republican majority to the United States Senate. President Reagan and the Republican Senate shared a philosophy quite different than their predecessors.

After Reagan's election as president, people who had previously fought and sued federal agencies over air pollution and land management and use policies became heads of those same agencies. The so-called Colorado mafia assumed control of the federal park machinery.

James Watt, chief legal officer of the Mountain States Legal Foundation, a public-interest law firm, became the Secretary of the Interior. The firm had been formed to check the power of the federal government whenever possible. Now its leader was placed in charge of federal land and resources.

Representative Ann Gorsuch, a Denver lawyer, who had battled the EPA over air quality policies and states rights in Colorado was appointed by President Reagan to be the Director of the EPA. A leading critic of federal air quality policies was now in charge of the federal program.

Robert Burford a Colorado rancher and Sagebrush "rebel" was appointed head of the Bureau of Land Management. From operating a ranch and fighting federal bureaucracy, he became the federal manager of 470 million acres.

Other people, with similar views, were appointed to high-ranking positions in various agencies impacting the environmental movement with views contrary to Carter's appointees. The backlash was in motion.

160

The change in federal policies was clearly seen in the absence of people wearing turtle neck sweaters and blue jeans in the halls of the Department of Interior. The Sierra Club members disappeared after the 43-year-old James G. Watt took office as the new Secretary of the Interior. The new uniform worn in the halls was western jeans and cowboy hats.

Within a month after Watt took office, federal management policies changed to:

1. Speed up land leasing for mining, oil, and gas
2. Eliminate park and recreation grants to cities and states
3. Start up the dormant dam building water development programs
4. Increase prospecting, cattle raising, and exploration

The park promoter of the nation, Representative Phillip Burton (Democrat—San Francisco, California) confirmed his alarm: "The worst nightmares of the environmental movement have become reality."

After Watt disclosed that he was terminating the grant-making functions of the heritage Conservation and Recreation Service, a federal agency, and transferring any remaining duties to the park service, the press asked him when the changes would take effect. Watt replied, "today." He eliminated the agency in one day. Watt was quoted by the *Los Angeles Times* (March 2, 1981) as saying, "When we know what we're going to do, we move quickly."

Watt further shocked the environmentalists by ordering that all park land acquisition be stopped immediately. President Reagan's proposed budget dictated the termination of the Land and Water Conservation Funds and additional unnecessary park purchases. The budget action would reduce park purchases from $282 million in 1980 to $45 million in 1982.

Many California park projects were curtailed. They included the following:

1. The cessation of the 150,000-acre Santa Monica Mountains National Recreation Area
2. The curtailment of additions to the Golden Gate National Recreation Area in San Francisco
3. The elimination of plans for a Big Sur National Scenic Area

Additional park acquisitions in other states will be stopped, such

161

as the Cuyahoga Valley National Recreation Area in Ohio; Cape Cod National Seashore in Massachusetts; the Appalachian National Scenic Trail; the Chattahoochee National Recreation Area in Georgia; and the New River Gorge National Recreation Area in West Virginia.

When reporters asked Watt about his cut-back action on the Golden Gate National Recreation Area, he responded:

> I think the city of San Francisco successfully dumped off a playground in the Golden Gate . . . They played one of the shrewdest games that any local government could do. Why we fell for that trick I'll never know. It's . . . a nice city playground that all of a sudden the taxpayers of America are supporting.

The announced cut-backs in funding of the Santa Monica Mountains National Recreational Area of $20 million in 1981 and $36.2 million in 1982 fermented an immediate reaction from park supporters in Los Angeles. A rally was led by Representative Anthony Beilenson (Democrat—Beverly Hills, California), Assemblyman Howard Berman, Los Angeles Mayor Tom Bradley, Councilman Marvin Braude, the Friends of the Santa Monica Mountains, the Sierra Club, and others.

The protestors claimed they would have at least 1,000 people at the rally. They could only muster a couple of hundred hard-core supporters. According to Peter Ireland of Concerned Citizens for Property Rights, "I think this shows they don't have that much support."

Representative Beilenson, angry at the Reagan administration's actions on the park, stated to the crowd: "Our problems here are typical of a larger national assault on the American environmental and conservation movement now being made by Mr. Reagan and Watt (Secretary of the Interior)." The crowd hissed and booed at the mention of Watt's name during the rally.

Secretary of the Interior James Watt, speaking to the North American Wildlife and Natural Resources Conference, advocated "orderly development of energy resources, greater access for public parks and wild lands and a greater role in managing federal land by state and local government." The latter was a "Sagebrush Rebellion" goal.

Watt said, "We will not throw the gates open and say: 'Here they are folks, help yourself'. We will manage the lands."

Concerned about the Carter administration's recent park purchases, Watt said that the park service had been pushed "to grab for more and more lands" and that they had "squandered" money on new parks and had let existing parks deteriorate.

Watt indicated that federal parks were purchased to be used by the public, not "to lock the treasures away from the people. The public's access to the park is being eroded."

He further stated, "We do not believe that the parks nor any of our resources should be held for the exclusive enjoyment of the elite."

President Reagan moved rapidly in changing the role of the Council on Environmental Quality in national affairs. After the appointment of A. Alan Hall, former Assistant Resources Secretary in California during part of Governor Reagan's two terms, the environmentalists were shaken again. All of the forty-nine staff members were informed that they would be fired within a few months. A total of sixteen staff members would operate the council.

The *Los Angeles Times* reported a staff member as saying the firing word went to "men and women, tall people and short people, fat ones and thin ones, people who had been there from the beginning . . . people of all ranks, everybody from the very top of the agency on down."

Environmental groups quickly formed new coalitions in response to Secretary Watt's comments that oil drilling may be permitted off the coast of Northern California and in the Santa Barbara Channel. A "stop the drilling" bipartisan coalition was organized to attack Watt's "arbitrary, capricious, and irrational" action.

Two dozen political, business, and environmental leaders met to announce their coalition. Five tracts totaling 1.3 million acres with a possible resource of 548 million barrels of oil and 621 million barrels of natural gas are at issue. Speaker of the California Assembly, Leo T. McCarthy indicated that if the public's outcry didn't convince the Reagan Administration, there would be an onslaught of lawsuits to tie up Watt's action until he leaves office.

Representatives of the boards of supervisors of counties affected, the Sierra Club, the Northern Central Coastal Commission, the Friends of the Earth, and the Pacific Coast Federation of Fisherman's Association attended the news conference.

A U.S. Supreme Court Reprimand

On March 24, 1981 the United States Supreme Court resurrected the constitutional guarantee of just compensation for the taking of private property. The same court that under President Carter had refused to tackle the issue of compensation in *Agins* v. *the City of Tiburon* (discussed earlier) addressed the issue of compensation, and confirmed the historic constitutional protection.

In the case of *San Diego Gas and Electric Company* v. *the City of San Diego* a majority of the court joined Justice Brennan in an unequivocal confirmation of the Fifth Amendment. The court affirmed the fifty-nine-year-old maxim of Oliver Wendell Holmes that if government "regulation goes too far it will be recognized as a taking." Justice Brennan continued:

> Public power regulations such as zoning ordinances and other land-use restrictions can destroy the use and enjoyment of property in order to promote the public good just as effectively as formal condemnation or physical invasion of property.

Moreover, the Court recognized the constitutional mandate that operates immediately in safeguard of individual rights:

> As soon as property has been taken, whether through formal condemnation proceedings, occupancy, physical invasion, or regulation, the landowner has already suffered a constitutional violation, and the self-executing character of the constitutional provision with respect to compensation is triggered. This court has consistently recognized that the just compensation requirement in the Fifth Amendment is not precatory: once there is a taking, compensation must be awarded.

In addition, the court denounced the remedy of invalidation (writ of mandate) offered by government and environmental lawyers as an alternative to compensation.

> Moreover, more invalidation would fall far short of fulfilling the fundamental purpose of the Just Compensation Clause. That guarantee was designed to bar the government from forcing some individuals to bear burdens which in all fairness, should be borne by the public as a whole.

Perhaps more important than the legal rhetoric was the concept of responsibility. Throughout the 1970s the environmental movement suggested a different standard of conduct for public urban planners than for the rest of our citizenry: they should be absolved from accountability as their liability would discourage the conduct of government. The Supreme Court has now disapproved that double standard, recognizing that financial liability will discourage government conduct in violation of individual rights. Finally, a confirmation of this work and of the direction of this message: "After all, if a policeman must know the Constitution, then why not a planner?"

It is difficult to explain the motivation by which the direction of American history is formulated. Yet for some inexplicable reason momentum was changed, and the resurrection and reaffirmation of constitutional rights stated. We are a nation of laws, but more importantly, a nation believing in the sanctity of individual rights.

The Future of the Environmental Movement

Despite this backlash away from radical and unrestrained conservation and environmental policy, the environmental movement is not going to go away. The environmental advocacy forces will apparently just change their direction for the 1980s. In the 1970s, they operated from the inside. In an article by Deborah Whitfield of the *Los Angeles Times,* November 18, 1980, she found in interviews with a number of environmental consumer groups after President Reagan's election that they planned to change their direction. Lobbying efforts were to switch from the White House and Capitol Hill to the state and local levels. Several groups planned to rebuild their contacts with other citizen groups and "to make greater use of the courts instead of federal regulatory agencies to advance their causes." Gregory A. Thomas, an attorney for the National Resources Defense Council stated to the *Los Angeles Times*: "We're going to have to revert to some of the tools of advocacy used in the past. It's time we started working with outsiders again instead of [government] insiders."

The day after President Reagan's victory in November 1980, the Consumer Federation of America began a letterwriting campaign urging its members to expand their contacts with senior citizens, neighborhood groups, labor, and tenant unions.

Ms. Whitfield quotes Tom Graff, Western Regional Counsel for the Environmental Defense Fund, as saying that environmental groups particularly "have focused too exclusively on Washington. We have a reorientation ahead of us." The groups contacted had unanimously supported President Carter and said they were worried both by Reagan's election and by the defeat of several liberal U.S. senators who were considered to be friends of environmental and consumer advocates. Tom Graff said, "We don't want people to think for a minute that the environmental movement is dead because Ronald Reagan is president."

After Ms. Whitfield's contact with consumer advocate Ralph Nader, she predicted that the federal courts "will be to the environmental consumer movement (in this decade) what they were to the civil rights movement in the 1950s and 1960s."

The *Times* quotes Carl Pope, Political Education Director for the Sierra Club, as saying: "We'll have to rely more and more on citizen action—direct litigation against industry—to enforce laws regulating toxic substances and water and air pollution."

Stephen Brobeck, Associate Director of the Consumer Federation of America further states: "The only way we can block all the anticonsumer initiatives we're expecting is by coalition—building an expansion of grass roots lobbying." Whitfield found that once environmental leaders regroup, "they expect to become more vocal in communities where energy development is being proposed." Environmental leaders planned to "wage more of their battles against air and water pollution and toxic chemical dumps before local and state agencies such as the California Air Resources Board instead of before the U.S. Environmental Protection Agency which Reagan has said needs to be reoriented."

The *Wall Street Journal* in its January 7, 1981 edition found similar evidence of changing environmental tactics for the future. Ray Vicker reported that several environmental group leaders were optimistic that the movement's underlying strength was healthy. There would be more cooperation among groups especially at the local level. Vicker quotes Janet Brown, Executive Director of the New York based Environmental Defense Fund: "I do not believe we should be unduly pessimistic. Public awareness of our air and water and land are widespread and growing."

The New York based National Resources Defense Council claims that its membership grew from 20,000 in 1975 to 46,000 by November 1, 1980. John H. Adams of the Defense Council said, "The environmental movement has maintained the momentum established during the early 1970 s."

The *Wall Street Journal* article found senators and representatives in Washington to be very familiar with environmental lobbying. One congressman told them, "You can't build a highway now without some group telling you that it will be harmful to a ladybug colony or an ant heap." The congressman added, "But don't quote me on that, I don't want to be on their hit list."

Time For Wiser Use of Our Resources

The election of Ronald Reagan and the national mandate for a balanced growth-oriented America forecast directional change for the environmental movement. That movement must become more balanced in approach and more sensitive to our energy, economic and housing needs. The movement must no longer threaten our economic productivity and the concept of private property ownership and individual liberty. National changes need to be made. Environmental goals, policies, and priorities must be reassessed and a new direction chartered that the nation understands.

Environmental Task Force Review

A federal task force should be assembled composed of leading constitutional attorneys, industrial representatives, public and private environmental planners, economists, and representatives of local government. This group should be given a targeted date to review and suggest simplification of duplicative, unnecessary, and complex federal environmental regulations. All federal environmental laws should be examined for a determination of their underlying goals, achievements, and failures. In instances in which the acts have failed or cases where the achievements have been outweighed by the detrimental impact upon economic productivity, local autonomy, unnecessary government organization, and individual rights, suggested legislative modification or repeal must be propounded.

Improving Environmental Regulations

When considering existing or proposed environmental control regulations, Congress must require that agency regulators measure both impact costs of the proposed regulations on the economy and consumers as well as the benefits.

Congress, not the EPA or any other agency, should set the standards and the desirable environmental and health levels or goals for the nation. This action would create national debate over desirable environmental goals that would be out in the open and subject to public scrutiny. In the past, zealous bureaucrats, not responsible to an electorate and under pressure from environmental special interests, set national standards.

A new system of simple but fair pollution controls should be devised by Congress in the form of a tax to achieve desirable standards. This action would make the control costs more visible to the public and apply the "price" of polluting more fairly to all polluters.

When taxpayers realize that environmental controls are actually adding $500 to $600 a year to their cost of living, they will take more interest in what the EPA, APCD, Coastal Commission and other agencies of the nation are doing. When taxpayers become more enlightened and understand that our inflation rate and "zero economic growth" are directly impacted by poorly conceived environmental goals and controls, action and a balanced approach will be obtained.

Our nation's scientists, inventors and government officials should be encouraged to be more creative in utilizing our resources, especially waste, for community energy needs. Environmental control regulations should be altered and softened if necessary to permit greater use of waste products, such as the burning of solid wastes to generate electricity, to heat water for homes and communities, or to develop usable gas byproducts. Present regulations hamper the use of waste for the public's benefit.

Federal Environmental Ombudsman

Congress should create an office of Federal Environmental Ombudsman whose sole function is to represent the interests of local and state governments and private enterprise in securing appropriate interpretation of federal environmental acts and report instances of improper federal administration of those acts to appropriate agencies and officials within the EPA and the Departments of Interior and Justice.

The increasing complexity of federal environmental laws necessitates the imposition of safeguards to insure that federal government officials do not take advantage of regulation complexity to further hamper local autonomy. There have been many examples of federal and local officials providing narrow interpretations of the Clean Air and Clean Water Act to unsuspecting boards of supervisors and city councils without informing them of the variety of alternatives that are open. Trusting and not realizing what the act actually said, legislative bodies were often herded unwittingly in an improper direction. The Federal Ombudsman, with expertise on environmental law, should be available to identify and investigate the conduct of federal officials and report improper conduct to enforcing agencies and Congress. The ombudsman could be part of the GAO structure.

Environmental Impact Report Process

The federal, state, and local government environmental impact report process (EIR) must be revised and streamlined significantly. Consideration should be given for requiring local governments to establish a community-wide environmental impact analysis program, warehouses of "banked" information, forming a basis of updated facts on such matters as air quality, traffic volumes, and construction in their region. These "environmental data banks" could include information on the economic and commercial needs of the community as well as physical data. Data "needed" should be incorporated into the regular project analysis process. Handled properly, this could alter much of the time spent by developers and planning staffs in preparing and reviewing EIRs. The present costly piecemeal approach used in most communities could be changed to a faster and more balanced fact-finding process for the community. The landowner or developer could thus initiate projects based on submittal of supplemental information to citywide information already on hand, rather than prepare costly and extensive studies only to be delayed by lengthy reviews.

The EIR should become a source of information for making decisions rather than a tool for the death knell of a project. The time review and public comment on EIRs should be significantly reduced and opposition limited to individuals who can demonstrate specific interest and potential harm by the project. There should be more control over unaffected special interest groups of a project who use their standing to delay or stop a project in its entirety.

Many irresponsible environmental and conservation groups out to achieve their goals are permitted under present federal and state legislation to stop or delay large projects for personal reasons at great expense to either government agencies or developers. It is important that these loopholes be closed and these groups held responsible for their actions, either through bonding requirements and/or assessments for legal costs imposed as a result of meritless nuisance lawsuits or protests.

Federal Park Acquisition

A complete reappraisal of the federal park practices is in order. That reappraisal should begin through Senate hearings. For the first time, extensive testimony should be submitted regarding national park practices and abuses. Department of Justice prosecutions should be made against those federal officials and employees who have knowingly and intentionally violated constitutional rights of property owners. Future congressional bills for park acquisition should be subjected to careful analysis as to the accuracy of appraisals and the extent to which the suggested appropriation is predicated on either "lowballing" or collaborative interactions between park officials and local governmental and environmental groups to achieve park-induced downzoning.

The Sagebrush Rebellion

The United States Congress should consider its long-term goals and uses to be made of federal lands, under the Bureau of Land Management, in the states. Should some land be transferred to state ownership? Should the western states have more control over useage or obtain actual ownership? Regardless of the transition, multi-use of federal lands must become a priority, as the economic and energy needs of the nation are stressed, but with logical and sensible environmental safeguards. This policy should permit, *with safeguards,* coal mining in the western states and additional mineral and oil exploration in previously untapped areas of Alaska's wilderness.

Coastal Resources

The coastal zones of our nation contain valuable assets which combine our population centers, commercial and economic accommodations and greatest natural resources. The use of properties within those zones must reflect a balance of all these needs. The final responsibility for management of resources should be in the hands of elected officials and not unaccountable bureaucracies. Stated simply, agencies such as the California Coastal Commission, essentially unsupervised, have no place in a free and democratic society and should be abolished without hesitation. If state agencies are necessary to administer entire coastlines, then the commissioners should be elected or the director be supervised by a state department head. In any event, federal funding should be conditioned upon compliance with constitutional conduct and curtailed in those instances such as California, where unrestrained bureaucracy has rendered a travesty of a democratic system.

Role of Government in Administering Resource Development

To return the country to a wiser and sounder federal system, it is suggested that the nation follow the policy recommendations of the Kestnbaum Commission: "Leave to private initiative all the functions that citizens can perform privately; use the level of government closest to the community for all public functions it can handle; utilize cooperative intergovernmental arrangements where appropriate to attain economical performance and popular approval; reserve national action for residual participation where state and local governments are not fully adequate, and for the continuing responsibility that only the national government can undertake."[79]

The Constitution

The United States Constitution embodies a concept of individual liberty without historic parallel. Our nation was founded in the belief that government existed to serve people and that state policy existed only at the pleasure of individual rights. Our judicial system is the guarantor of that concept, that no one state goal or policy could result in the taking of individual liberty, that property was "earned liberty" and could not be taken without due process and just compensation.

There are those who would change this system, who believe in more government regulations than are necessary, who await a day of government ownership and control of all our property, business, economy, and life. For those who share a different belief in the sanctity of individual rights, in the inherent value of private property ownership and our historic concept of freedom, we seek a restoration of individual liberty and an end to "The Taking."

Appendices

Appendix A
Major Federal Environmental Legislation

Federal Lands Management

In an attempt to manage federal lands better, Congress passed the following federal acts: the Federal Land Policy and Management Act of 1976 and the Forest and Rangeland Renewable Resources Planning Act of 1974 as amended by the National Forest Management Act of 1976. There were other acts concerned with resources such as mining, forestry, and grazing. Although these were primarily concerned with federal land, government policies had an impact on private land owned in and near federal property, especially when the federal government owns over one-third of the United States.

Pollution Control Legislation

Concern for the environment in the areas of air, water, and coastal areas brought about a number of far-reaching acts in the 1970s. These included: the Coastal Zone Management Act of 1972, the Clean Air Act of 1972 (amended in 1977), the Clean Water Act of 1972, the Safe Drinking Water Act, the Resource Conservation and Recovery Act, and the Surface Mining Control and Reclamation Act. All but one of these acts contained requirements for planning that have an impact upon local government and private property.

172

Federal Planning and Environmental Coordination Acts

To better coordinate federal, state, and local activities related to the environment, several acts were passed to improve planning and coordination. These included: The National Environmental Policy Act of 1969, Fish and Wildlife Coordination Act, National Historic Preservation Act, Water Resources Planning Act, and the A-95 Planning Coordination Procedures. There were other executive orders such as Flood Plain Management Executive Order 11988 (1977) and Protection of Wetlands Executive Order 11990 (1977).

Other Federal Acts Having Land Use Impact

Other programs by the federal government that had a major impact on land use at the state and local level concerned transportation, agriculture, urban development and housing, and power plant siting. These programs were manifested by the Federal Air Highway Act, Urban Mass Transit Act of 1964 (with 1974 amendments), Surface Transportation Assistance Act of 1978, Airway Development Act of 1970, Housing and Community Development Act of 1974, the Disaster Relief Act of 1974, and Energy Reorganization Act of 1974. The federal government also impacted environmental planning through the Federal Energy Regulatory Commission, the Tennessee Valley Authority, and its various agricultural programs through the Soil Conservation Service, Rural Electrification Administration, and the Farmers' Home Administration.

Federal Programs Protecting Natural Resources

To protect natural resources of the nation, various programs and legislation were passed concerned with cultural resources, rivers, wilderness areas, parks and recreational land, fish and wildlife, water resources, and flood plains.

Cultural Resource Protection

New laws in the 1970s concerning cultural protection included the Preservation of Archeological and Historical Data Act of 1974, the Surface Mining Control and Reclamation Act of 1977, and the Tax Reform Act of 1976. Other acts previously passed also gave direction to federal policy on cultural resource protection.

Preservation of Wetlands

The first federal wetlands protection legislation was passed in 1972 by Congress entitled the Federal Water Pollution Control Act Amendment.

Wilderness Areas

Although a national wilderness preservation system was created by Congress in 1964, this system was enhanced by the Federal Land Policy Management Act of 1976.

Management of Flood Plains

The federal government's power over managing flood plains was expanded with the Flood Disaster Protection Act of 1973 and various flood insurance programs.

Wild and Scenic Rivers Legislation

Although the Wild and Scenic River Act was passed in 1968, the power of the act has been increased with various interpretations by Congress and the Secretary of the Interior.

Parks and Recreation

With the passage of the National Park Service Mining Activity Act of 1976, Congress limited mining activity on federal park land. Other executive orders and reorganization action by the Department of Interior has changed the direction of the National Park Service and caused a severe problem to private landowners within the park system.

Fish and Wildlife and Endangered Species

Through the passage of the Fish and Wildlife Coordination Act and Endangered Species Act of 1973, federal agencies must insure that no endangered species will be harmed by a federal project. Citizens' suit provisions are included that make it possible by environmental groups to definitely hold up a government project.

Water Conservation Programs

Through the Water Resources Council, the federal government has strengthened its water conservation programs throughout the country.

Appendix B
Major Federal and State Legislation Impacting Local Government and Private Land-Use Planning Authority

The environmental legislation of the 1970s had a significant and severe impact on both the rate of growth and cost of development in the United States. The major acts and their impact on local government and private property owners is described below. The federal legislation and the followup state and local action are described in order for the reader to understand the local impact. Only the major acts and policies of the federal and state government in California having impact on local government and private property are described. There are many more acts, of course.

National Environmental Policy Act of 1969

The first federal legislation that dealt with environmental issues was the National Environmental Policy Act, signed into law on January 1, 1970. This Act required federal agencies to prepare environmental impact studies on proposals for legislation and other major federal actions significantly affecting the quality of the human environment. Congress declared that the Act was "to promote efforts which will prevent or diminish damage to the environment." The Act established the Council on Environmental Quality (CEQ) as advisor to the President on environmental issues. In 1971, CEQ published guidelines on the intent of the act. The Environmental Protection Agency in 1972 published policies and procedures for identification and analysis of the environmental impact of federally proposed or assisted actions and the preparation and processing of Environmental Impact Studies. An EIS, as they are called, analyzes the anticipated impact of a project on the environment such as air, land use, water, plant, and wildlife.

California Environmental Quality Act, 1970

As a result of environmental concerns, the California State Legislature quickly enacted the Environment Quality Act (CEQA) in 1970. CEQA stated that environmental protection shall be considered in all decisions made by local agencies with the fundamental objective being defined as using "feasible measures to mitigate or avoid adverse environmental impacts." The act requires that before a project can be approved or disapproved, the public agency must take certain action regarding CEQA. Each jurisdiction must conduct an "initial study" of a project to determine whether it may have a significant effect on the environment. If the initial study results in a finding that the project will not have a significant impact on the environment, a jurisdiction can prepare and file a negative declaration. This contains a description of the project and a statement that the project will have no significant effect on the environment. Assuming a city follows all proper procedures, the project can then be approved. If there is some evidence, however, that the project may have a significant impact or effect on the environment, an Environmental Impact Report (EIR) must be prepared. There are further requirements that all projects of statewide or areawide environmental significance shall be submitted to the state for review, even if the state has no power of approval.

As a result of administrative guidelines and decisions by courts, CEQA has jurisdiction over more than just projects. They now have jurisdiction over land use controls such as general and specific plans, rezoning, annexations, zoning development permits, and subdivision approvals. The environmental planning process has become a lengthy, costly and complicated process. Environmental groups have been able to question and challenge Environmental Impact Reports to such an extent that they can tie up a project for years. Various public agency projects such as major highways and airport expansions have been held up for years because of challenges to the Environmental Impact Report by environmental groups.

When an EIR has been prepared, it is normally reviewed by a governmental agency committee and then heard at a public hearing before a planning commission and the legislative body and certified by them before a project, private or public, may be adopted. The EIR has become in California an important function of the decision making process for any private or public project. As a result of CEQA, new firms specializing in environmental matters have developed throughout California. New courses were taught at universities and colleges and degrees offered specializing in environmental affairs. A new "profession" developed, not only in California but throughout the United States.

1970 Federal Clean Air Act Amendments and Clean Air Act of 1977

With rapidly deteriorating air quality throughout the country, Congress passed the Clean Air Act of 1970 which gave each state the primary responsibility for assuming air quality control within its jurisdiction. The Environmental Protection Administrator was authorized under the Clean Air Act to divide the United States into Air Quality Control Regions which were appropriate for the attainment and maintenance of air quality standards. Along with the establishment of air quality control regions, the Act established "National Ambient Air Quality Standards" (NAAQS) to be achieved. The Clean Air Act further required that all regions of the country that exceed the NAAQS prepare and implement a plan to achieve and maintain the NAAQS as "expeditiously as practical" but no later than December 13, 1982. There are possible extensions to 1987 with approval from the EPA administrator. To get an extension, the state must demonstrate that all Reasonable Available Measures (RAM) have been implemented to control emissions.

The Clean Air Act further required that each state prepare a detailed State Implementation Plan (SIP) that demonstrated how the specific air standards (NAAQS) were to be met. Any county or region within the state that exceeded the NAAQS in 1975–85 was a nonattainment area and had to prepare an Air Quality Management Plan (AQMP) within its SIP. The plan had to show how the regional strategy could be implemented to attain and maintain the NAAQS. If a state fails to submit a satisfactory plan, EPA has the authority to write its own plan and force the state to implement it.

The federal government carries a big stick in administering the Clean Air Act. If a region does not achieve air quality standards within the given deadline, the "crossover" system comes into play, and federal grants to a community under the Clean Air Act, Federal Highway Act, water and sewer programs could be jeopardized. The Environmental Protection Agency has the power to deny transportation projects, prohibit major new sources of industrial development and put a moratorium on construction of sewage treatment plants. Compliance to the Clean Air Act, therefore, has an impact on land use and the growth of industry, residential areas and transportation systems of a community.

Air Pollution Control and the State

The agency in California responsible for the preparation of the State Implementation Plan (SIP) is the California Air Resources Board (ARB). All regional Air Quality Maintenance Plans (AQMP) must be approved by the California Air Resources Board. Any plan submitted to it must prove that it includes all "reasonable and available" methods to meet and maintain state air standards. Air Quality Management Plans can be revised by the ARB. Ventura County, like many others, was selected as a region that exceeded the NAAQS. It was required to prepare an Air Quality Management Plan (AQMP).

After approval of an AQMP by the State ARB for inclusion in the State Implementation Plan, the SIP is submitted to the Environmental Protection Agency for its approval. The responsibilities of the EPA in acting on SIPs are very specific. If the state submits an inadequate plan or fails after sixty days to revise the plan found by the EPA administrator to be inadequate, the plan will not be approved by the EPA administrator.

Air Pollution Control and the County—Ventura County Air Pollution Control District

In Ventura County, the Board of Supervisors acts as the County's Air Pollution Control Board and is responsible for the development of an Air Quality Management Plan (AQMP) for the county. The Air Pollution Control District (APCD) is the administrative arm of EPA and the Board of Supervisors. After the Board of Supervisors has approved an AQMP, acting as the county's Air Pollution Control Board, the plan is submitted to the California Air Resources Board (ARB) for inclusion in the State Implementation Plan. An important purpose of an AQMP is to insure that anticipated future growth and development in a state Air Resources Board District, to the maximum extent feasible, be consistent with the goal of maintaining required air quality standards. There is a requirement that the AQMP contain control strategies affecting land use and transportation. The purpose is to improve air quality by reducing vehicle miles traveled and emission generated.

In Ventura County, the AQMP prepared by the Ventura County Air Pollution Control District made it clear that Ventura County has not achieved the National Ambient Air Quality Standard and will not achieve it by the 1982 deadline, even though the "regional strategy" is immediately implemented. The county requested an extension to 1987 to achieve the ozone and carbon dioxide standards. This was requested because it did not seem possible through reasonable available control measures to attain the NAAQS by 1982.

In Ventura County, the AQMP points out that the air pollution problem is closely associated with the problems of land use, transportation, and the availability of water and power.

The Air Quality Management Plan contained an implementation schedule on stationary source measures, mobile source measures, transportation control measures, and land use development measures. The land use development measures contained policies that would affect the citing of station emission sources and the magnitude and distribution of mobile and area sources through more effective management of the timing, quantity, location, density, and type of development in the cities and the county.

By APCD regulating the type and location of industrial development, the future population growth of a community can be regulated. In other words, the creation of jobs as well as land use locations can be controlled indirectly by the APCD.

Clean Water Act—1972

In 1972, Congress passed the Federal Water Pollution Control Act Amendments known as the Clean Water Act. Its major purpose was restoring and maintaining "the chemical, physical and biological integrity of the nation's waters." The act stipulated a national goal "that discharges of pollutants be eliminated by 1985." It further stated a national water quality goal, wherever attainable, providing for the protection of and propagation of fish, shellfish, and wildlife, and providing for recreation in and on the water to be achieved by July 1983. To achieve this goal, it was deemed necessary to survey water quality and establish water quality standards in the United States.

Section 208

Within the Clean Water Act, under Section 208, the governor of each state must identify areas with "substantial water quality control problems." After this identification, each state is required to select "a single representative organization, including elected officials from local government" to operate "a continuing areawide waste treatment management planning process." The Environmental Protection Agency is required to approve any plans prepared and certified by the state. Planning funds are made available to local jurisdiction under Section 208. Only cities or jurisdictions designated as a 208 management agency or projects included in the plan can receive federal construction grant funds, once the 208 plan is approved.

Although the Environmental Protection Agency (EPA) could not enforce plans, they could withhold permits for control of waste discharges or grants for construction of waste treatment facilities not in conformance with 208 plans. It therefore was important to jurisdictions anticipating growth of their communities to adhere to the requirements of Section 208.

The state agency responsible for each 208 planning process in California is the State Resources Control Board. It has responsibility for certifying plans and designating a management agency to implement plans for each planning area. Under the Resources Control Board were Water Quality Control Boards.

Although Section 208 is entitled "Areawide Waste Treatment Management," its provisions have more implications and impact than indicated. As Ventura County discovered, "areawide 208 planning" really means "regional planning."

Water quality control until 1972 was a local concern. Each community treated its own wastewater, primarily in individual treatment plants. There was little concern with plans for nonpoint sources of pollution such as urban runoff and sediment from construction or agricultural activities.

The Clean Water Act, through Section 208, changed local control rapidly. The 208 Act called for water quality planning with new strategies that included:

(1) Land use and growth management techniques.
(2) Areawide planning for water quality supersedes local planning. Areawide planning is dictated or conducted by either a state or, in most cases, a regional planning agency.
(3) Management agencies are designated as 208 plans. These agencies must have full authority to implement the plan.
(4) Nonpoint sources of pollution must be regulated by the plan.

Section 208 requirements have important land use implications as they require land use and growth management techniques. The plan can control or regulate the location of pollution-generating activities. As the 208 plan must identify all sewage treatment facilities for an area's needs for twenty years and establish priorities of construction, the plan can determine the growth potential of an area. The 208 plan requires a program "to regulate the location, modification, and construction of any facilities which may result in any discharge." This gives a community authority to deny construction and development permits of treatment plants, offices, industrial plants, stores, homes, and other buildings that discharge sewage if the potential discharge threatens to exceed existing treatment capacity.

Regional Water Quality Control Board

The Regional Water Quality Control Board is the state/regional operating arm of the Clean Water Act and EPA. By regulating the discharge requirements for point sources of water pollution, consistent with a basin water plan point, and its recommendations to the State Water Resources Control Board or state funding of local treatment facilities, the RWQCB can influence the location and type of urban development. The ability to influence state funding can in turn influence the growth of a community's population. In critical air basins, the state will not provide state funding for treatment facilities until there is consideration of the project's growth-inducing impact. In areas where air quality does not meet state and federal standards, the State of California generally attempts to avoid stimulating growth.

Ventura Regional County Sanitation District

As VRCSD has authority to plan and implement sewerage treatment facilities, it can influence the location and development and population growth. VRCSD is guided and influenced by the Clean Water Act, EPA, and the RWQCB. For instance, VRCSD can determine if the location of a treatment facility in an undeveloped area will encourage the area's growth and development. VRCSD can influence the type of development occurring in a given location by their requirements for pretreatment of affluent to be disposed of in a facility and by the capacity of the plant. If VRCSD requires reduction of the capacity of a sewer plant, it can control the number and variety of housing projects that could be built in a given area.

Ventura County Flood Control District

The VCFCD can prevent or limit the type of development in flood hazardous areas. This can be done through the implementation of the Water Course Ordinance and other flood control requirements. The VCFCD can also impose development standards for projects to be constructed. The conditions of their requirements can be extensive as well as requiring the setting aside of large areas of land for flood control projects. VCFCD is also guided and influenced by funding and regulations of various federal acts and EPA.

Special Districts

Special districts that provide water and sewerage services probably have the greatest influence over the location and type of development and the growth management of any given area. Without water or sewers, most communities can grow very little. Within Ventura County, there are twelve water districts, all of which impacted land use planning and the projected growth of the community. Special sewer districts have an impact similar to the VRCSD except that their influence is on a local or smaller area rather than on a regional or countywide area.

There are other special districts for lighting, roads, etc., that have an influence on growth but to a minor extent compared to water and sewer districts.

County Health Officers

County Health Officers in recent years have been influencing the growth and location of development through applying various federal and state health standards to protect the public health. Many health officers have been generating their own standards and criteria without support from existing regulations. This is usually done by establishing standards for septic tank use in larger lot type subdivisions.

Federal Highway Act of 1970

Under the Federal Highway Act of 1970, the Highway Trust Fund was established from which most states' and communities' highway construction money is derived. Funds are made available to jurisdictions following the mandates of the act. Under the Trust Fund, the federal government provides 90 percent of the construction costs for the interstate system and approximately 70 percent of funds for other major road work.

To receive funds, communities must adhere to a number of planning and land use considerations. There is an "Environmental Action Plan" requirement for all federal aid systems. The plans must consider economic, social, and environmental effects, including:

- Air, noise, and water pollution
- Destruction or disruption of manmade and natural resources, aesthetic values and the availability of public facilities and services
- Adverse employment effects and tax and property value losses

- Injurious displacement of people, businesses, and farms
- Disruption of desirable community and regional growth

All federally associated projects require an "Action Plan" be prepared. Action Plans must provide for citizen input through public hearings and are subject to a multilevel review within the Federal Highway Administration (FHWA). Highway planning must also be consistent with State Implementation Plans prepared under the Clean Air Act.

Comprehensive long-range planning in urban areas is required. The Secretary of Transportation is directed *not* to approve programs "unless he finds that such projects are based on a continuing comprehensive planning process carried on cooperatively by states and local communities." These plans must be continually revised and submitted annually to FHWA for approval. There are other requirements including environmental factors and adherence to the Federal Highway Beautification Act that must be considered. As highways directly affect land use and community growth, local jurisdictions are greatly impacted by federal policies relating to the ground rules for obtaining funds for planning and construction.

California Transportation Act

To coordinate state activities with those of the Federal Highway Act of 1970, the California Transportation Act was passed. The primary objectives of CTA were to: (1) de-emphasize road construction in favor of multi-modal balance between highway and mass transportation systems; (2) develop a statewide comprehensive transportation plan; (3) develop a state plan through a "bottoms up" planning process which relied principally upon substate transportation plans. The goal was to prepare a state plan that achieved a coordinated and balanced statewide transportation system, including mass transit, highways, aviation, and highway systems "consistent with the state's social, economic, and environmental needs and goals." The plan is to be updated each year for two years after legislative approval and then every second year thereafter.

State plans are submitted to the State Transportation Board for approval. The California Department of Transportation (Caltrans) is responsible for development of the plan. The state plan, however, is built from the various regional transportation plans developed by regional transportation agencies as approved by Caltrans. Caltrans appointed the Southern California Association of Governments (SCAG) as the state-designated TPA for the Southern California region. In Ventura County, the local regional government, Ventura County Association of Governments, in cooperation with the Public Works Department, the Air Pollution Control District, Planning Departments, transit operators, and other agencies in Ventura County, is responsible for preparing the "subregional" plan.

As the Federal Highway Act of 1970 required consistency between federally aided highways and state plans for implementing regional air quality standards, the State Highway Agency (Caltrans) was required to follow appropriate procedures to insure that the planning and construction of highways was consistent with the State Implementation Plan (SIP) for air quality.

A-95 Review Process

When the Intergovernmental Cooperation Act of 1968 was passed, it directed the president to "establish rules and regulations governing the formation, evaluation and review of federal programs." Seven major land uses and items were required to be addressed by the rules: appropriate land uses, development and conservation of natural resources, balanced transportation systems, outdoor recreation and open space, areas of unique natural beauty and historical and scientific interest, planned community facilities, and standards of design.

As a result of circular S-95, a clearinghouse system was established whereby federal grant applicants notify the clearinghouse of their intent to apply for federal assistance. The system is used to identify potential conflicts and problems. The clearinghouse also provides a mechanism for state and local review of Environmental Impact Statements.

Southern California Association of Governments

The Southern California Association of Governments (SCAG) acts as the clearinghouse for a five-county region, including Ventura County. Processing a public project through SCAG is yet another administrative item that costs additional money for staff and processing time. SCAG has a tendency to reinforce local general plans and growth control policies.

State Review of Local Plans and Projects

Traditionally, the state has had limited authority in the review process of planning elements prepared by local jurisdictions. In California, the state's review of local planning is limited, for example, to open space and housing elements prepared in accordance to state-developed regulations. There are also state-legislated mandated guidelines for the preparation of a general plan. Local agencies also report annually as to their compliance with guidelines.

Recently, however, the California State Office of Planning and Research has assumed authority not legally permitted and has threatened to stop the issuance of all building permits in counties not complying with the office's mandates.

Local Agency Formation Commission

In the late fifties and early sixties in California, many cities had imperialistic growth goals and expanded in an erratic manner. To prevent haphazard urban expansion into prime agricultural land, the state legislature passed the Knox-Nesbitt Act and established countywide control of annexations to cities and special districts by a Local Agency Formation Commission (LAFCO). Another level of government was established to regulate land use. Five members were appointed to LAFCO's in each county. They consisted of: (1) two members representing the county, appointed by the board of supervisors from its membership; (2) two members representing the cities in the county, each of whom shall be a city officer appointed by a city selection committee; and (3) one member representing the general public appointed by the other four members of the commission.

The legislature gave LAFCO the authority to review and approve or disapprove the annexation of territory to cities or special districts. They were not to impose conditions which would directly regulate land use or subdivision requirements. The formation of LAFCOs did dampen and bridle the often erratic five and six-mile, 200-foot wide annexations of some choice property for industrial or commercial purposes to "improve" a community's tax structure.

In order to act on an annexation proposal, the LAFCOs in California consider many factors. They consider population density, land use, proximity to other populated areas, natural conditions, projected growth, governmental services, conformity with LAFCO policies on orderly development, conformity with city and county general and specific plans, and the "sphere of influence" established for cities and special districts.

The result was a separate hearing body and a new bureaucratic staff to review proposed public and private projects. LAFCO, in reality, has power to regulate and influence the location and type of land use development and urbanization of communities. LAFCO further regulates population growth and densities by controlling the expansion of an urban service area or special district providing services within the community.

The California Coastal Commission

With the creation of the California Coastal Commission and six regional commissions, another planning jurisdiction was established that had impact on Ventura and communities along the California Coast. The Coastal Commission had authority, in general, 3,000 feet inland from mean high tide. The cities' and county territory along the coast came under the jurisdiction of the California Coastal Commission. The Coastal Commission planners had their own ideas as to how the coastal area, which contains some of the most expensive land in the county, should be planned and utilized. The commissions had authority and used it to override government plans and local projects that had been approved locally.

The Coastal Commission not only controlled land use but managed growth within the coastal permit zone by regulating or limiting the type, density, and location of development through the planning and permit system.

The requirement that private builders or developers and homeowners process their plans through the Coastal Commission added another administrative cost and delay to the project. Many of the conditions the Coastal Commission placed on projects were unwarranted and costly to applicants. Hundreds of projects were abandoned due to the unfair conditions of the commission.

The actions of the commission for the good of the coast actually harmed the environment. By limiting, over-regulating, over-conditioning, delaying, and stopping housing projects, commission action drove up the cost of land and housing.

Other Public and Semipublic Agencies
Influencing Land Use Planning and Growth

Utility companies, school districts, telephone companies, etc., also influence planning and growth of a community by their availability to expand facilities and services to areas. In general, utility companies respond to public demand rather than influence where growth should take place.

Appendix C

Sources for Figures

Figure 4. Various California Coastal Commission reports.

Figure 9. Office of the Federal Register, *1977/78 United States Government Manual,* Washington, D.C., U.S. Government Printing Office, 1977; and Louis M. Kohlmeier, *The Regulators,* New York, Harper and Row, 1969, appendix, pp. 307–12.

Figure 10. Subcommittee on Economic Growth and Stabilization of the Joint Economic Committee, Congress of the United States, *The Cost of Government Regulation,* Washington, D.C., U.S. Government Printing Office, April 1978, pp. 57–59.

Figure 11. Wright, Deil, "The Administrative Dimensions of Intergovernmental Relations." Draft for *Contemporary Public Administration,* Thomas Vocino and Jack Rabin, eds. (New York: Harcourt, Brace Jovanovich, Inc., July 1979); Mosher, Frederick, C. and Poland, Orville, F., *The Costs of American Governments: Facts, Trends, Myths,* New York: Dodd, Mead and Company, 1964, p. 162; and ACIR staff computations.

Figure 12. Jacob, Herbert and Vines, Kenneth N., eds. *Politics in the American States, A Comparative Analysis,* 3rd Edition, Boston: Little, Brown and Company, 1976, p. 21.

Figure 13. Office of Management and Budget, "Federal Government Finances," unpublished tables, January 1976, pp. 51–53, and *1981 Budget,* Special Analysis 1-1, p. 251.

Figure 15. Fiorina, Morris P., *Congress: Keystone of the Washington Establishment,* New Haven: Yale University Press, 1977, p. 93; and the Public Interest, Number 47, National Affairs, Inc., New York, Spring 1977, p. 50.

Figure 16. Lovell, Katherine, et al., *Federal and State Mandating to Local Government: Impact and Issues,* Riverside, CA: University of California, 1979 draft, p. 71.

Figure 24. Rutledge, Gary L., "Pollution Abatement and Control Expenditures in Constant and Current Dollars, 1972-77," *Survey of Current Business,* Washington, D.C., Bureau of Economic Analysis, February 1979, p. 15.

Figure 26. Ellison, Richard. "Growth Management," Urban Land Institute, San Diego, CA, 1979.

Figure 27. Ibid.

Figure 28. Ibid.

Notes

CHAPTER ONE

1. Anderson, Kent. "People of Blue Ridge."

CHAPTER TWO

2. *The Los Angeles Times.* January 17, 1981.
3. From the Forest Service the following areas were examined: Nicolet National Forest (Wisconsin); Eleven Point Wild and Scenic River (Missouri); Spruce Knob-Seneca Rocks National Recreation Area (West Virginia); Lake Tahoe Basin (California and Nevada); Whiskeytown-Shasta-Trinity National Recreation Area (California); Chattahoochee National Forest (Georgia); Chattooga Wild and Scenic River (Georgia, North Carolina and South Carolina); Rogue Wild and Scenic River (Oregon); and Sawtooth National Recreation Area (Idaho). In addition, the GAO visited and inspected the following sites of the National Park Service: Voyageurs National Park (Minnesota); Lower St. Croix National Scenic Riverway (Minnesota and Wisconsin); Grand Teton National Park (Wyoming); Cape Cod National Seashore (Massachusetts); Golden Gate National Recreation Area (California); Yosemite National Park (California); Big Cypress National Preserve (Florida); Blue Ridge Parkway (North Carolina and Virginia).
4. Of this total, almost 700,000,000 acres were always in public domain and not privately owned in the past.

5. *The Federal Drive to Acquire Private Lands Should Be Reassessed,* GAO Report, December 14, 1979, p. 9.

6. Staff memo to William Whelan, Director of the National Park Service, January 8, 1980.

CHAPTER THREE

7. *Environmental Quality,* Tenth Annual Report of the Council on Environmental Quality. Washington, D.C.: U.S. Govt. Printing Office, Dec. 1979.

8. North Coast Regional Commission, with headquarters in Eureka and exercising jurisdiction over the counties of Del Norte, Humboldt, Mendocino; North Central Coast Regional Commission, with headquarters in San Rafael and exercising jurisdiction over the counties of Sonoma, Marin and San Francisco; Central Coast Regional Commission with headquarters in Santa Cruz and exercising jurisdiction over the counties of San Mateo, Santa Cruz and Monterey; South Central Coast Regional Commission with headquarters in Santa Barbara and exercising jurisdiction over the counties of San Luis Obispo, Santa Barbara and Ventura; South Coast Regional Commission with headquarters in Long Beach and exercising jurisdiction over the counties of Los Angeles and Orange; and San Diego Coast Regional Commission exercising jurisdiction over the county of San Diego.

9. Nine elements were to be considered by the staffs of the Regional State Commissions: (1) the marine environment, (2) coastal land environment, (3) geology of the Coastal Zone, (4) appearance and design, (5) recreation, (6) energy, (7) transportation, (8) intensity of development, and (9) government organizations, government powers, and funding necessary to carry out the coastal plan.

10. The planning area along the coast was defined as the Coastal Zone and consisted of the land and water area "extending inland to the highest elevation of the nearest coastal mountain range except for Los Angeles, Orange and San Diego Counties; the inland boundary of the Coastal Zone shall be the highest elevation of the nearest coastal mountain range or five miles from the mean hightide line, whichever is the shorter.

11. Excluded from this zone were the Farallon Islands and the San Francisco Bay.

12. California Public Resources Code 27001.

13. An issue of statewide significance.

14. Although smaller applications for such items as tree or brush removal, fence repair, or minor house alteration usually received "over the table" administrative approval, any significant construction (e.g., house addition and beyond) needed full public hearing approval.

15. The State Commission staff, following receipt of the Notice of Appeal, prepared a staff report for the Commission's information in determining whether a substantive state issue existed. If the Commission votes to hear the appeal (finding a substantive issue), the staff then prepares recommendations and findings concerning the application, a synopsis of the project, and possible conflicts with policies of the Coastal Act, and the case is heard anew, a *de novo* hearing.

16. From 1977 through December 1979, 1,454 appeals were sent to the State Coastal Commission (see chart entitled "State Commission Action of Appeals, January 1977–December 1979"). Of the appeals received, 1,032 were processed. Only 388 appeals were actually heard by the Commission out of 1,454 received. In 644 cases, the decision of the Regional Commission was upheld without a hearing, and of the 388 appeals actually heard, 299 were approved and 89 denied. One hundred twenty-three appeals were withdrawn. It is interesting that 55 percent of the appeals filed were from groups, organizations, and individuals other than the applicant.

17. The Coastal Act defined an LCP as follows: "Includes a local government's land use plan, zoning ordinances, zoning district maps, and, where required, other implementing actions applicable to the coastal zone." The most important part of the LCP is the land use plan. It indicates the kinds, location, and intensity of land and water uses and proposed resource protection and development policies to accomplish the Coastal Act objectives. Assisting in implementing the land use plan are the zoning ordinances, maps, and policies. The zoning ordinances are a major tool in carrying out the policies and provisions of the land use plan.

18. This total does not reflect accounting for various state agency time and personnel dedicated to support of Coastal Commission activities such as Department of Justice or Department of Parks and Recreation.

19. This practice was finally curbed by the California Legislature in reform legislation adopted in mid-1979.

20. Hearings held to review the conduct of the Coastal Commission

by the Federal Office of Coastal Zone Management (January–February 1980).

21. *Star Free Press.* January 31, 1979.
22. *Coastal News.* Vol. 3, No. 1. Jan.–Feb., 1980.

CHAPTER FOUR

23. Dubos, Rene. *The Wooing of Earth.* (New York: Charles Scribner's Sons, 1980.)
24. Young, James Sterling. *The Washington Community: 1820–1828.* (New York: Harcourt Brace and Jovanovich, Inc., 1966), p. 31.
25. "Land and Natural Resources Management: An Analysis of Selected Federal Policies, Programs and Planning Mechanisms." Report to the President's Interagency Task Force on Environmental Data and Monitoring Programs, prepared by the Council on Environmental Quality and Resource and Land Investigations Program, U.S. Geological Survey, U.S. Department of Interior.
26. Ibid.
27. Ibid.
28. "A Crisis of Confidence and Competence." *The Federal Role in the Federal System: The Dynamics of Growth,* Advisory Commission on Intergovernmental Relations, Washington, D.C., July 1980.
29. *Summary and Concluding Observations: The Intergovernmental Grant System: An Assessment and Proposed Policies,* Advisory Commission on Intergovernmental Regulations A-62, pp. 67–68.
30. Ibid.
31. "Revenue Sharing Funds Distributed." News Release, October 11, 1979. U.S. Department of Treasury, Office of Revenue Sharing, Washington, D.C.
32. Krier, James E. and Ursin, Edmond. *Pollution and Policy: A Case Essay on California and Federal Experience with Motor Vehicle Air Pollution, 1940–1975.* (Berkeley: University of California Press, 1977), p. 297.
33. Schultze, Charles L. "The Public Use of the Private Interests." (Washington, D.C.: The Brookings Institution, 1977), p. 4.

34. Masotti, Louis H. "Toward a Viable Urban Future in a Society of Limits: Possibilities, Policies, and Politics." Paper presented at annual meeting of American Political Science Association, New York, August 31, 1978, p. 2.

35. *Tidewater Constructor,* June 1979.

36. *California Journal.* March 1981, pp. 102-103.

CHAPTER FIVE

37. *Environmental Quality,* The Tenth Annual Report of the Council of Environmental Quality. Washington, D.C.: U.S. Government Printing Office, December 1979.

CHAPTER SIX

38. Cooke, Alistair. *Alistair Cooke's America.* (New York: Alfred A. Knopf, 1974), p. 122.

39. A complicated analysis of human history which attributes our only known realities to the forces of change, transformation, and encounter of matter.

40. Marx, Karl and Frederick Engels. *Manifesto of the Communist Party.*

41. Liberalism reflected a clear and unequivocal alternative to the communal society and, more particularly, the individual associated dogma thereafter introduced by Marx. Thus liberalism balanced Communism's dialectic attack on religion, family, and property with the concept of the inalienable rights of man and the basic dignity of humanity.

42. Locke, John. *Second Treatise,* Chapter 5, Section 27.

43. Fifth Amendment, United States Constitution.

44. *Pennsylvania Coal* v. *Mahon* (1922) 260 U.S. 393.

45. *Miller* v. *McKenna* (1944) 23 Cal. 2d, 774,783.

46. *House* v. *Los Angeles County Flood Control District* (1944) 25 Cal. 2d, 383,391.

47. *Arastra Limited Partnership* v. *City of Palo Alto* (1975) Northern District of California (401 Federal Supplement 962).

48. *Southern Pacific Company* v. *Railroad Commission* (1939) 13 Cal. 2d, 89, 117; see also *Peacock* v. *County of Sacramento* 271 Cal. App. 2d, 845.

49. Berger, Michael M. "You Can't Win Them All—Or Can You?" *California Bar Journal,* January–February Edition, p. 16.

50. *Transcentury Properties, Inc.* v. *State of California* (1974) 41 Cal. App. 3d.

51. *Klitgaard and Jones, Inc.,* v. *San Diego Coast Regional Commission* (1975) 48 Cal. App. 3d, 99.

52. Berger, Michael M. "You Can't Win Them All—Or Can You?" *California Bar Journal,* January–February Edition. (See extensive instances cited.)

53. Briggs v. State of California, 159 Cal. Reporter 390 (1979).

54. Drummond, Judge Ralph, Superior Court of Monterey County, California.

55. Approximately eight months thereafter, a jury of her peers and judge would award Mrs. Briggs several increments of damage, including the fair market value of her property, interest, damages, and attorneys and court costs in a sum in excess of $6.5 million.

56. Jackson, Robert. *The Case Against Nazi War Criminals.* (New York: Alfred A. Knopf, 1946), p. 22.

57. Ibid., p. 22.

58. *Ibid.,* p. 25.

59. Quoted from decree issued January 14, 1936, as appears in *Documents on Nazism, 1919–1945,* introduced by Jeremy Noakes and edited by Geoffrey Pridham. (New York: The Viking Press, 1945), p. 273.

60. Ibid., p. 266.

61. Ibid., p. 266.

62. Ibid., p. 272.

63. Ibid., p. 272.

64. Ibid., p. 273.

65. Hayek, F. A. *The Road to Serfdom.* (Chicago: University of Chicago Press, 1944.)

66. Ibid., p. 55.

67. *Documents on Nazism,* 1945, p. 265.

CHAPTER SEVEN

68. Frieden, Bernard. *The Environmental Protection Hustle.* (Cam-

bridge, Massachusetts: M.I.T. Press, 1979.)

69. Ibid.

70. *Environmental Quality.* The Tenth Annual Report of the Council of Environmental Quality. Washington, D.C.: U.S. Government Printing Office, December 1979.

71. Ibid., pp. 75–78.

72. Ibid.

73. Ibid.

74. Crandall, Robert. "Is Government Regulation Crippling Business?" *Saturday Review,* January 20, 1979.

75. Ibid.

76. Ibid.

77. Ibid.

78. "Final Summary Report," U.S. Committee of Paperwork. Washington, D.C.: U.S. Government Printing Office, October 3, 1977, p. 5.

79. "Growth Restrictions and New Home Prices," Construction Industry Research Board, May 1978.

80. "Growth Management," *Urban Land,* January 1979.

81. *Government Regulation and Housing Costs.* The Rutgers University Center for Urban Policy Research. New Brunswick, New Jersey, June 20, 1977.

82. *The Cost of Environmental Protection.* The Rutgers University Center for Urban Policy Research. New Brunswick, New Jersey, 1976.

83. Seidel, Stephen R. *Housing Costs and Government Regulations Confronting the Regulatory Maze.* The Rutgers University Center for Urban Policy Research. New Brunswick, New Jersey, 1978.

CHAPTER EIGHT

84. "Final Report of the Commission on Intergovernmental Relations," House Document 198, 84th Cong., First Session. Washington, D.C.: U.S. Government Printing Office, 1955, p. 6.